JAMES LAMBERT (1758-1847)

An Elaboration of His American Revolutionary War Service in the
Virginia Militia and Virginia Line Based Upon a Comprehensive Analysis
of His Pension File No. R 6099 and Further Extensive Research.

by

GEORGE ROBERT LAMBERT

authorHOUSE®

AuthorHouse™
1663 Liberty Drive, Suite 200
Bloomington, IN 47403
www.authorhouse.com
Phone: 1-800-839-8640

First published by AuthorHouse 3/20/2009

ISBN: 978-1-4389-0621-8 (sc)

Library of Congress Control Number: 2008910177

Printed in the United States of America
Bloomington, Indiana

This book is printed on acid-free paper.

INTRODUCTION

I am writing at age 75 this Introduction on the 250th birthday anniversary of my third great-grandfather, James Lambert, who was born on 25 March 1758 near Little Pipe Creek, in Frederick (now Carroll) County, Maryland.

My serious research of my Lambert family line started almost ten years ago at the National Archives, Washington, D.C., in August 1998, when I reviewed for the first time the James Lambert Pension File on microfilm.

My interest in identifying an American Revolutionary War soldier in my Lambert family line was influenced significantly by the two most important women in my life, namely, my dear mother, Velma Lou (Lucille) (Jones) Lambert and my beloved wife, Mary Virginia (Alling) Lambert. My mother had identified the Revolutionary War soldiers in her Jones family line and my wife had identified the Revolutionary War soldiers in her Alling family line. As a result, both my mother and my wife were active members in Chapters of The National Society of the Daughters of the American Revolution (DAR). In fact, I became a member of The National Society of the Sons of the American Revolution (SAR) because of the research my mother had done on her Jones family line.

It was the passions my mother and my wife had for their Revolutionary War patriots that inspired me to identify a Revolutionary War soldier in my Lambert family line so that my descendants and others could join in the future DAR and SAR Chapters through their Revolutionary War patriot ancestor in their Lambert family line.

When I started this project almost ten years ago, all I knew about my Lambert family ancestors who preceded my first great-grandfather, John N. Lambert, was that they lived near Vevay in southern Indiana.

The completion of this project was also motivated by my realization that I have reached the sunset years of my life on earth and by my collection and notation of the following inspirational quotations:

(1) **"The greatest use of life is to spend it for something that will outlive it."** (This quotation by William James appeared in a Hallmark Treasures Booklet entitled "Beautiful Thoughts" given to me and my family by my mother during the Easter Week of April 1971.)

(2) **"Christians plant trees even though they will not be around to enjoy the shade with future generations."**

(I frequently have heard statements to this effect by Reverends Victor A. Ulto and Monsignor Cosmos Saporito of the St. Bernadette Catholic Church, Port St. Lucie, Florida. Their references were usually to the construction of a new church and parish center.)

(3) **"The man who feels no sentiment for the memory of his forefathers, who has no regard for his ancestors, or his kindred, is himself unworthy of kindred regard or remembrance."**

(This quotation attributed to Daniel Webster appeared on some material my wife received as a member of the Illinois Chapter of the Daughters of Founders and Patriots of America.)

(4) **"Show me the manner in which a nation or community cares for the dead and I will measure with mathematical exactness the tender mercies of the people, their respect for the laws of the land, and their loyalty to high ideals."**

(This quotation attributed to William Gladstone was copied by my wife from a wall mural at the Garden of Memories Cemetery, north of Muncie, Indiana, and the location of the grave sites of my uncle, Ernest E. Quick, and his wife and my dear aunt, Marjorie Alice (Lambert) Quick.

(5) **"People will not look forward to posterity who never look backward to their ancestors."**

(This quotation from Edmund Burke was copied from a wall mural at the Allen County Public Library, Fort Wayne, Indiana.)

(6) **"For what is the worth of human life, unless it is woven into the life of our ancestors by the records of history?"**

(This quotation from Marcus Tullius Cicero was also copied from a wall mural at the Allen County Library, Fort Wayne, Indiana.)

Finally, I have many Lambert family relatives to thank for their assistance in helping me compile pertinent information about our Lambert family line. They include the following:

Adele Bowen, Webster City, Iowa

Margaret L. (Goody) Christy, West Liberty, Iowa

Jennie J. Hott, Franklin, West Virginia

Hoyt H. Harmon, Jr., South Chatham, Massachusetts

Bonnie (Sollars) Johnston, Cincinnati, Ohio

John Boyd Lambert, Lake Forest, Illinois

John Ray Lambert, Muncie, Indiana

Linda Joanne Lambert, Upland, Indiana

Marilou (Cecil) Lambert Dickey, Upland, Indiana

Tutt Lambert, Loveland, Ohio.

It is my hope that this analysis and elaboration of the Revolutionary War service of my 3rd great grandfather, James Lambert, will be informative and of interest to the readers, especially to my children, Robert Allen Lambert, Ann Holt (Lambert) Balnek and James William Lambert, as well as to my grandchildren, Brittany Marie Lambert, Bjorne Ann Balnek, Kristina Liv Balnek, Connor Jordan Lambert and Ryan James Lambert. Hopefully, one or more of them will not only continue the research on his or her Revolutionary War soldier and ancestor, James Lambert, but will be motivated to keep the Lambert family history up-to-date.

This compilation is dedicated to the two most important ladies in my life; namely, my wife, Mary Virginia (Alling) Lambert and my mother, Velma Lou (Lucille) (Jones) Lambert, and to my 3rd great grandfather, James Lambert, and all of his ancestors and descendants.

TABLE OF CONTENTS

Analysis of the
James Lambert Pension File Documents

My third great-grandfather, James Lambert, made extraordinary efforts in his eighties to document his background and experiences for the bureaucrats in the War Office of the United States, Washington, D.C., hoping that they would agree that he was entitled to a pension based upon his military tours of duty during the American Revolutionary War. Although he did not live long enough to convince them that he was a Revolutionary War soldier, James Lambert was successful in recording his background and experiences for the benefit of his posterity and others.

I had the opportunity to review and copy microfilm documents in the James Lambert Pension File No. R6099 at the National Archives, Washington, D.C., in August of 1998 and seven years later at the Allen County Public Library, Fort Wayne, Indiana, in August of 2005. I also reviewed copies of such records sent to me on January 30, 2007, by Lineages, 175 West 200 South, Suite 1000, P.O. Box 417, Salt Lake City, UT 84110, which it had obtained from National Archives Microfilm Publications.

Since microfilm records are very difficult to read, I transcribed to the best of my abilities the following documents found in Pension File No. R6099 which I have included in the Appendix:

(1)   Statement of Lemuel Hungerford (23 Jul 1841)

(2)   Declaration of James Lambert (18 Nov 1841)

(3)   Amended Declaration of James Lambert (13 May 1844)

(4)   Amended Declaration of James Lambert for a Pension (21 Aug 1844)

(5)   Letter to the Hon. O. B. Ficklin (6 Jun 1848)

(6)   Letter from T. R. Young (5 Jan 1850)

(7)   Letter from Francis A. Dickins (19 Mar 1852)

(8)   Letter from Francis A. Dickins (31 Jan 1853)

(9)   Power of Attorney (14 Mar 1854)

(10)   Letter from G. H. Voss (13 Jun 1855)

Summary of Declaration of
James Lambert (18 Nov 1841)

On 18 November 1841, James Lambert personally appeared in Open Court before the Probate Court of Dearborn County, State of Indiana, located at that time in the town of Wilmington and he stated that

*"...on the 25 day of March 1842 he will be eighty-five (eighty-four) years old, that he was born in the State of Maryland, that he is now a resident of said County (**Dearborn**) and has been for the 27 years last past, that he has lived in Virginia, Maryland, Pennsylvania, Ohio and Indiana, . . . that at the age of nineteen at the town of Augusta in Virginia, he was drafted as a militia man for the term of three months, that he rendevous'd at Shenandoah, Virginia, and thence marched to Richmond, Virginia, and from thence was taken by water to West Point, New York, where when his term of three months expired he volunteered for the term of two years and after remaining there a winter and a summer he was marched to and was in the Battle of Cowpens and thence was marched to one of the Moravian towns on the Yadkin River where he was regularly discharged which he has lost, that he served as aforesaid two years and three months in the army of the revolution, the reason why he never applied for a pension is that he never needed a pension until now, the name of his Major was Guy Hamilton, Captain name Spencer, Sergeants names John . . . . , Hildepeny, William Bryan, Col. Hilliard or Hilyard, that his memory is defective and further says not."[1]*

Notes in Pension File No. R6099 show that the pension authorities in Washington sent a letter on 8 Jan 1842, suggesting that James Lambert needed to specify his tours of service in more detail.

Comments on the Amended Declaration of James Lambert (13 May 1844)

In response, an Amended Declaration was prepared by James Lambert and others in their heroic efforts to meet the aggravating demands of the pension bureaucrats in Washington, D.C.

---

1   See Appendix, Item 2, p. 121.

On 13 May 1844, James Lambert personally appeared in Open Court before the Hon. James Duncan, sole Judge of the Ripley County Probate Court, State of Indiana, and James Lambert stated under oath that he was age 86 on the 25th day of March 1844 and a resident of Dearborn County. The following reason was given for his appearance that day in Ripley County rather than Dearborn County:

"...He lives about thirty miles from Lawrenceburg the present County seat of Dearborn, where the Courts of the said County are holden, and he resides not more than fifteen miles from this Court, the Road from his residence to this Court is much better than to Lawrenceburg, and he is wholly dependent on the kindnesses of his neighbors for the means of coming to Court to make his declaration and it was much easier for him to get a friend to bring him to this Court than take him to Lawrenceburg . . . "[2]

A person of the 21st century can better understand the hardships of traveling to Versailles in the 1830s and 1840s by reading the following:

1830 Trip from Lawrenceburg to Versailles

S. A. Ferrall wrote about his trip from Lawrenceburg to Versailles. Ferrall said "We left Lawrenceburg early and traveled until the horse became jaded. We camped out near Wilmington the first night, got an early start the second day on a newly finished roadway. The builder's contract stated that no stump be left higher than 15 inches in the new road. We spent the second night at a backwoodsman's cabin. He was from Kentucky and had recently cleared 18 acres of land. He and his very ugly squaw lived in their comfortable cabin, and fed us venison and stewed squirrel. They said deer were fairly plentiful, but bear were becoming scarce. The third day we proceeded to Versailles."[3]

Thus, the trip between Lawrenceburg and Versailles at that time took three days. One can easily visualize that a horse would become "jaded" after a full day of being steered around tree stumps up to 15 inches high in the roadway so that the buggy and its wheels would clear such obstructions. We also learn that a local backwoodsman from Kentucky had recently cleared 18 acres for farming purposes. He lived in this wilderness with his Indian squaw wife in a cabin he had probably built by himself, and their meals included cooked and stewed wild animals, such as, bear, deer and squirrel.

---

2   See Appendix, Item 3, p. 123.
3   Smith, Alan F., <u>Tales of Versailles</u>, 1999, Four-Sep Publications, Milwaukee, WI 53212, p. 12.

We can understand that James Lambert used very good judgment in traveling just fifteen miles to Versailles rather than the thirty plus miles to Lawrenceburg.

Mr. John Ruby, a clergyman residing in the County of Ripley, and Isaiah W. Robinson, an attorney also residing in said County, both certified that:

"...we are well acquainted with James Lambert ... that we believe him to be eighty-six years of age, that he is reputed and believed in the neighborhood where he resides to have been a soldier of the Revolution and that we concur in that opinion."[4]

James Lambert gave the following answers to questions propounded by the War Office:

(1) He was born on Pipe Creek near Hagerstown, Maryland, on the 25th day of March 1758.

(2) The record of his age is recorded in his father's family bible then located in Nelson County, Kentucky.

(3) He was first called into service against the Indians at Wilson Station in Tiger (Tygart) Valley on the Monongahela. He moved to Rockingham (Augusta) County, Virginia, on the Potomac, residing there the whole war. He then resided in Kentucky and Ohio until he resided the last 14 years in Dearborn County.

(4) The first tour he volunteered, the second he was drafted, the third he was a substitute for Jacob Ellsworth and the fourth he volunteered.

(5) He well remembered the Riflemen commanded by Gen. Morgan, the Cavalry commanded by Col. Washington, also Col. Howard Regiment, Col. Lee, Col. Lynch, Col. Nock Regiment of Militia and Capt. Morton Company.

(6) He received a written discharge at Broad Ford on Adkin River signed by Col. Hillyard but it was lost on the person of William Bennett.[5]

Judge James Duncan declared the following opinion:

"...after the investigation of the matter, and after putting the interrogatories prescribed by the War Department that the above named applicant (James Lambert) was a Revolutionary Soldier and served as he states ... "[6]

---

4   See Appendix, Item 3, p. 128.
5   Ibid., p. 129.
6   Ibid., p. 128.

It should be noted that at the time these documents were prepared James Lambert was considered to be a weak and feeble old man in his eighties and he was attempting to remember the details of events that he experienced as far back as 70 years. No small challenge at his age, but James Lambert met the challenge with all the mental capacity and determination he could muster.

The Honorable James Duncan, Justice of the Ripley County Probate Court

James Duncan was born in Pennsylvania in 1804. It is believed that around 1830, James and his brother, William, moved from Pennsylvania and came to Ripley County, Indiana. There James met Sarah Shook and they were married on 5 May 1831. Sarah's father, David Shook, was the local Justice of the Peace in Versailles, Indiana, Ripley County.[7]

On 1 July 1836, James Duncan purchased land in Ripley County, being one of the original land owners.[8]

To the union between James and Sarah Duncan were born seven children. They being: Lydia Ann, born in 1833, Amanda Louisa, born in 1835, Sarah Jane, born in 1838, Mary Francis, born in 1843, Margaret Elizabeth, born in 1844, James William, born in 1847, and Isaiah Edward, born in 1855.[9]

James Duncan left Ripley County, Indiana, sometime in the middle of the 1860's and located on a farm in Oakwood Township, Vermillion County, Illinois.[10]

The 1850 U. S. Federal Census lists the James Duncan family of seven in Versailles, Johnson Township, Ripley County, Indiana. He was born in Pennsylvania, age 39, Justice of the Peace, and value of real estate owned was $300.[11]

The 1860 U. S. Federal Census lists the James Duncan family of seven in the same location. He was listed as a farmer age 54.[12]

---

7   Lane History Page, http://hometown.aol.com, p. 9 of 14, on 8/14/2008.

8   Ibid.

9   Ibid.

10 Ibid.

11 1850 United States Federal Census - Ancestry.com, http://search.ancestry.com, p. 1 of 1, on 8/14/2008.

12 1860 United States Federal Census - Ancestry.com, http://search.ancestry.com, p. 1 of 1, on 8/14/2008.

The 1870 U. S. Federal Census lists the James Duncan family of three in Oakwood Township, Vermillion County, Illinois. He is listed as a farmer age 66.[13]

The 1880 U. S. Federal Census lists James Duncan, age 74, with his wife Sarah, age 69, living with their son, James W. Duncan, age 33, and his family of five, in Urbana, Champaign County, Illinois. It is also reported that the parents of James Duncan were both born in Ireland.[14]

Conrad Overturf, Clerk of the Court, and John Hunter, Deputy Clerk of the Court

The first county Courthouse was built in 1821 and the first settlers of Ripley County included Conrad Overturf and John Hunter. By 1849 Versailles contained 27 brick and 38 frame houses with a population of 350[15]

The 1840 U. S. Federal Census listed in Johnson Township, Ripley County, Indiana, the C. Overturf family of 3 males and 7 females, and the John Hunter family of 8 males and 6 females. The oldest male age for each family was in the age range of 50 and under 60.[16]

The 1850 U. S. Federal Census listed the Conrad Overturf family of seven at the same location, indicating that Conrad Overturf was born in Kentucky about 1795 and his occupation as Recorder of Ripley County with the value of real estate owed at $2,000.[17]

John Ruby and Isaiah W. Robinson, Certificate Witnesses

The 1840 U. S. Federal Census listed the John Rubey (Ruby) family of 4 males (the oldest male being in the 40-50 age range) and 5 females in Johnson Township, Ripley

13 1870 United States Federal Census - Ancestry.com, http://search.ancestry.com, p. 1 of 1, on 8/14/2008.

14 1880 United States Federal Census - Ancestry.com, http://search.ancestry.com, p. 1 of 1, on 8/14/2008.

15 More About Ripley County, http://www.countyhistory.com/ripley/more.htm, p. 1 of 2, on 8/14/2008.

16 Ancestry.com - 1840 United States Federal Census, http://search/ancestry.com, p. 1 of 1, on 8/15/2008.

17 Ancestry.com - 1850 United States Federal Census, http://search.ancestry.com, p. 1 of 1, on 8/15/2008.

County, Indiana, and the Isah (Isaiah) W. Robinson family of one male (20-30 age range) and two females in York Township, Switzerland County, Indiana.[18]

The 1850 U. S. Federal Census listed the Isiah (Isaiah) W. Robinson family of three males and three females in Versailles, Johnson Township, Ripley County, Indiana. Isaiah was said to have been born in Vermont about 1814 and his occupation was "Lawyer."[19] Since John Ruby was not listed in this Census for Ripley County, Indiana, he must have moved his family out of said County in the late 1840's.

History of Dearborn County

Since James Lambert was a resident of Dearborn County, Indiana, at the time these documents were prepared, the reader should better understand the history of Dearborn County, Indiana.

A historical summary on Dearborn County reads as follows:

"Dearborn County, located along the Ohio River in Southeastern Indiana, is the third oldest county of the Indiana Territory and thus contains some of Indiana's earliest and most significant architecture. The county's northern boundary is Franklin County, and the eastern is Hamilton County, Ohio. The Ohio River and Laughery Creek form the southern boundary, and the western boundary is Ripley County–the county line being the Greenville Treaty line arranged by General Anthony Wayne in 1795.

Geographically, Dearborn County is a mixture of flatlands in the northwest and rolling hills divided by several creeks forming long valleys throughout the county. The principle waterways are the Whitewater River in the northwest corner of the county, the east and west forks of Tanners Creek, North and South Hogan Creeks, and Laughery Creek.

Dearborn County was organized in 1803 (March 7) by Governor William Henry Harrison, who named it after General Henry Dearborn, at that time the Secretary of War under President Thomas Jefferson. All or part of six other counties were carved from the original Dearborn County with the present boundaries being established in 1845. Official organization of most of the fourteen townships of Dearborn County occurred in the 1830's and 1840's. The last township, Washington, was organized in 1852.

---

18 Ancestry.com - 1840 United States Federal Census, http://search.ancestry.com, p. 1 of 1, on 8/15/2008.

19 Ancestry.com - 1850 United States Federal Census, http://search.ancestry.com, p. 1 of 1, on 8/15/2008.

The town of Lawrenceburg was established as the county seat in 1803, a year after its original plat was laid out by Samuel Vance, James Hamilton, and Benjamin Chambers. In 1810 a two-story frame courthouse was built. Destroyed by fire in 1826, it was replaced by a new building which served until 1836 when the county seat was moved to the town of Wilmington where a new brick courthouse was erected. Wilmington remained the county seat for only eight years with Lawrenceburg permanently retaining its position in 1844 (April 1). The present County Courthouse was built in 1870.

Settlers began entering Washington, Center, and Lawrenceburg Townships in the late 1790's. Most of them moved down the Ohio River from homes in the eastern United States. There were numerous land entries through the Federal Land Office in Cincinnati beginning in 1801, occurring primarily in the lower creek valleys and along the Ohio River bottomland.

In 1820 the Manchester Pike was established as part of Indiana's Internal Improvements Program, and in 1823 a road was constructed from Madison through Vevay, Rising Sun, and Aurora, to Lawrenceburg. From 1836 to 1843 the Whitewater Canal was built through Dearborn County. River and canal trade dominated the county's commerce until the construction of the Ohio and Mississippi Railroad in the 1850's.

From the 1820's to the 1870's there was a steady immigration of European settlers into Dearborn County. German Catholics and Lutherans settled in the St. Leon and New Alsace areas of Kelso Township as well as portions of Jackson and Caesar Creek Townships. English immigrants settled in Caesar Creek, York, Harrison, Logan, and Lawrenceburg Townships, and Irish immigrants moved to Sparta, Clay, Washington, and Manchester Townships. Many of them came from such eastern states as Maine, Pennsylvania, New Jersey, and Delaware. The mixture of European settlers provided an interesting source of town names such as Wilmington, Yorkville, Guilford, and New Alsace. Examples of early immigrant commercial efforts remaining in the county include the Zix Brewery near New Alsace, Miller's Mills in Sparta Township on South Hogan Creek, and the Hayes Branch Saw and Grist Mill located in Clay Township.

The population of Dearborn County grew from 4,424 in 1815 to 23,000 by 1890. Early in its history the county had a strong agricultural base; in 1910 there were more than 2,200 farms with an average of 83 acres each. Many industries were built throughout the nineteenth century including distilleries, furniture, glass, pump, and coffin companies, as well as a boat building company. . . ."[20]

---

20 Dearborn County History, http://www.dearborncounty.org/history/dchistory.html , on
    10/25/2006. (Information provided by Dearborn County Interim Report).

FIRST MILITARY TOUR OF DUTY
VOLUNTEERED FOR THREE MONTHS IN 1774 AT AGE 16
BATTLE OF POINT PLEASANT ON 10 OCTOBER 1774

According to James Lambert's account, his first military tour of duty commenced near the first day of June in 1774 when he volunteered for three months, serving against the Indians under the leadership of Colonel Lewis, Major Hamilton, Captain Skidmore, Lt. Colonel Rafe Stewart, Ensign William White, and 1st Sergeant James Stewart, a brother of Lt. Colonel Stewart. He was marched from Wilson Station in the Tiger (Tygart) Valley on the Monongahela River through the wilderness to the mouth of the Kanawha River under the guide of Joseph Friend and also Captain Frogg who commanded in the right wing at the Indian Battle and was killed in that engagement. James Lambert crossed the Cheat River, Laurel Fork and Glady Fork to the Kanawha and down the river to the mouth and he returned nearly the same route.

The following interesting personal observations by James Lambert about this Indian Battle are quoted from the Amended Declaration of James Lambert (13 May 1844):

"... he was in a severe engagement with the Indians about three hundred whites were killed and wounded but how many of the Indians could not be ascertained as the warriors to save the scalps of the fallen would drag them to the Ohio and throw them into the stream. This battle was a hard one, the Indians were defeated, but with great losses to the whites. Sergeant Stewart was killed and this applicant (James Lambert) received several Balls through his clothes. This engagement commenced near Sunrise and lasted all day. He served for full three months when he returned home to his father at Wilson Station, this was in his seventeenth year (his 16th birthday was on 25 Mar 1774), and the first of September 1774 or in a few days of that time at all events he served full three months when he was verbally discharged ...."[21]

---

21 See Appendix, Item 3, pp. 123 and 124.

On July 24, 1774, Lord Dunmore wrote Colonel Andrew Lewis and his brother, Colonel Charles Lewis, requesting that they raise sizable forces to join him at the mouth of the Great Kanawha in a campaign against the Indians. Colonel Andrew Lewis held a meeting at his home on August 12th, and he was joined by Colonel William Preston, Colonel William Christian, and Colonel William Fleming. They agreed to enlist troops and to rendezvous on the Greenbrier River by the end of August. The southern division under Colonel Andrew Lewis first assembled at Camp Union, now the location of Lewisburg, on August 27th, and more troops arrived each day thereafter. The force consisted of three groups; the Augusta County Regiment under Colonel Charles Lewis, the Botetourt County Regiment under Colonel William Fleming, and the Fincastle County Battalion led by Colonel William Christian. In addition, there were independent companies, such as, the Culpeper Minute Men, 40 strong, under Colonel John Field; the Dunmore County Volunteers, also 40 in number under Captain Thomas Slaughter; Bedford County Riflemen, 44 strong, under Captain Thomas Buford; and 27 Kentucky Pioneers brought by Captain James Harrod. The army at Camp Union was one of the most remarkable ever assembled on the American frontier. They were a typical backwoods group, both officers and soldiers. They wore fringed hunting shirts, dyed yellow, brown, white, or red; ornamented shot bags and powder horns hung from broad belts. They had caps or soft hats, moccasins, and coarse woolen leggings reaching halfway to the thigh. Each carried his flintlock, tomahawk, and scalping knife. The caliber of the army was such that Theodore Roosevelt wrote: *"Although without experience of drill, it may be doubted if a braver or physically finer set of men ever got together on this continent."* Colonel William Preston said of them: *"This body of militia being mostly armed with rifle guns, and a great part of them good woodsmen, are looked upon to be at least equal to any troops for the number that have been raised in America."*[22]

The first ten days of September were spent organizing and supplying around 1,490 troops, more than Colonel Andrew Lewis had expected. Colonel Charles Lewis left with his Augusta County Regiment on September 6th to build a small storehouse at the mouth of the Elk River and to make canoes for transporting supplies to the Ohio River. He took with him 500 packhorses carrying 54,000 pounds of flour and beeves, besides a quantity of salt and some tools. Colonel Andrew Lewis left Camp Union on September 12th with his Botetourt troops and several of the independent companies together with 200 packhorses laden with flour and a drove of beeves. He left Colonel William Christian and his Fincastle men to await the return of the packhorses taken

---

22 Colonel William Fleming in Dunmore's War, 1774, http://wvculture.org/HISTORY/ journal.wvh/wvh3-2.html , pp. 2 and 3 of 13, on 2/24/2008.

by Colonel Charles Lewis. The march from the camp on the Greenbrier to the junction of the Great Kanawha and Ohio Rivers was a difficult one, for there was no trail of any kind and few white men had ever gone down the Kanawha Valley. The route was 160 miles of trackless forest, rugged and mountainous. Wagons were impossible, and all the provisions were transported on packhorses. On September 23rd, after marching 108 miles in twelve days, the army joined Colonel Charles Lewis and his men at the junction of the Elk and Kanawha Rivers. A week was then spent making more canoes, storing some of the supplies in a magazine built for them, and completing all arrangements for the final phase of the journey. Colonel William Fleming wrote that the men loaded 18 large canoes on September 29th and they resumed their march on September 30th. The troops were formed into two columns, the Botetourt troops on the right and the Augusta troops on the left. On October 5th, the troops had to form one column to pass between the hills and the river. On October 6th, the troops arrived at the bottom land which extended nearly four miles to the junction of the Kanawha with the Ohio. The Virginians camped at Point Pleasant for the next three days. On October 9th, Colonel William Christian's forces of about 200 men were only 15 miles from the encampment at Point Pleasant.[23]

There is a map of the Kanawha River through the counties of Fayette, Kanawha, Putnam and Mason. This map shows the junction of the Elk River and the Kanawha River near Charleston. It also shows the junction of the Kanawha River and the Ohio River near Point Pleasant.[24]

The Shawnee Chief, Cornstalk, after an unsuccessful effort to pacify his people, gathered his warriors to attack the white men at Point Pleasant before they could join Lord Dunmore. After dark on October 9th, the warriors crossed the Ohio River in 79 rafts three miles above Point Pleasant. Early on the morning of October 10th, two soldiers left camp to hunt deer. After going about two miles, they sighted a large number of Indians who fired at the hunters and killed one of them. The survivor ran back to the camp to alert the troops. Colonel Charles Lewis was ordered to advance with 150 men along the foot of the hills on the right and Colonel William Fleming led a similar group along the Ohio River bank on the left. About 3/4ths of a mile from the camp, the Indians attacked first the right line and then the left line. Colonel Charles Lewis fell mortally wounded at the first attack and Colonel William Fleming was seriously wounded shortly later. As a result, both lines retreated until Colonel

---

23 Ibid., pp. 3, 4, and 5 of 13.
24 Kanawha River Central Map, West Virginia, http://www.rootsweb.ancestry.com, p. 2 of 2, on 5/9/2008.

John Field arrived with reinforcements. Colonel William Christian heard the firing and hurried to advance his troops, but he did not arrive on the scene until midnight, when all was over and there was silence except for the groans of the wounded.[25]

The following information on the Battle of Point Pleasant appeared on the American Revolution History Archives web site, sponsored by the Sons of the American Revolution:

"The 'Boston Tea Party' of December 16, 1773, annoyed the British king and parliament and led to the formulation and passage of . . .

The Quebec Act—This extended the borders of Quebec southward to the Ohio River and west to the Mississippi (the area that is now Wisconsin, Michigan, Illinois, Indiana, and Ohio) and extinguished the claims that a half-dozen American colonies had on that land based on their previous royal charters. The Quebec Act emboldened Indian tribes along the Ohio River to attack the European settlements on the frontier (which was part of Virginia at the time). John Murray (Lord Dunmore), the royal governor of Virginia, sent two military columns to the frontier. Colonel Andrew Lewis—with 1,122 Virginia militiamen from Augusta, Botetourt, and Fincastle counties—marched overland and on October 6 arrived at Point Pleasant (40 miles northeast of what is now Huntington, WV). Murray's army went by way of Pittsburgh and was to join Lewis's militia at Point Pleasant, but Murray delayed his troops, hoping that Chief Cornstalk would annihilate Lewis's militia units. A Shawnee chief, Blue Jacket, visited Murray's camp on Oct. 9th. The next day, October 10, 1774, Chief Cornstalk, with an Indian force of over a thousand Shawnees and Mingos, launched a surprise attack on the colonial militia at Point Pleasant. The battle was fierce, but the attack was repulsed. If Colonel Lewis's men had not defeated the Indian force, the outcome of the Revolution might have been different, since Virginia would have been too busy protecting the frontier to participate in the Revolution. Because of this the U.S. Congress in 1908 recognized the Battle of Point Pleasant as the first battle of the American Revolution."[26]

The following is quoted from Soldiery of West Virginia:

---

25 Colonel William Fleming in Dunmore's War, 1774, http://wvculture.org/HISTORY/journal.wvh/wvh3-2.html, p. 5 of 13, on 2/24/2008.

26 American Revolution History Archives - Point Pleasant, The Battle of Point Pleasant by Ralph Nelson, based on notes from Richard L. Carpenter, Tennessee Society SAR, http://www.sar.org/cnssar/liberty/military/ptplesnt.htm, p. 1 of 2, on 8/29/2005.

". . . Here (Fort Gower) Dunmore awaited the arrival of intelligence from the Southern Division of the army which he had ordered General Andrew Lewis to collect at 'Camp Union' on the Big Levels of Greenbrier,–now Lewisburg, West Virginia. This Division was composed of a Regiment from Augusta county, commanded by Colonel Charles Lewis; a Regiment from Botetourt county under Colonel William Fleming; a Battalion from Fincastle county, at whose head was Colonel William Christian . . . . This Division left Camp Union, in September, and proceeded to the Ohio river on which, at the mouth of the Great Kanawha, on Monday, October 10th, 1774, the greater part of it was engaged in the battle of Point Pleasant, the most desperate struggle ever waged between white men and Indians in America. . . .

In the Southern Division under General Lewis there were thirty company organizations; and of these the rolls of eleven have been preserved. . . ."[27]

In the Augusta County Regiment the only list was for Captain William Nalle's Company of Volunteers and James Lambert was not included in that list. Thus, James Lambert must have been with one of the nineteen company organizations that did not have a preserved roll of its members.[28]

A Partial List of the Officers Killed and Wounded at the Battle of Point Pleasant, Oct. 10, 1774, included Col. Charles Lewis and Col. Jno. Field under the heading "Field Officers Killed", and John Skidmore was included under the heading "Captains Wounded". A Partial List of Officers and Men at the Battle of Point Pleasant, Oct. 10, 1774, included Andrew Lewis as the Brig.-General, Commanding, and Colonel Charles Lewis and Colonel John Field were listed again as killed. Under the heading "Sutler", John Frog(g) was also listed as killed.[29]

A search on Dunmore's War listed 45 soldiers from various counties, including 15 from Augusta county, nine from Fincastle county, eight from Botetourt, six from Frederick county, three from Culpeper county, two from Bedford county, one from Hardy county and one from an undetermined county. The following 19 militia soldiers in that list were killed in action on 10/10/1774 at Point Pleasant, West Virginia:

---

[27] Lewis, Virgil A., <u>Soldiery of West Virginia</u>, 1978 Reprint, Chapter III, West Virginia Soldiers in Lord Dunmore's War, pp. 29 and 30.

[28] Ibid., p. 30.

[29] Crozier, William Armstrong, <u>Virginia County Records</u>, Genealogical Publishing Co., Inc., 1986. Baltimore, Maryland, Vol. II, Virginia Colonial Militia 1651-1776 - Lord Dunmore's War, 1774, pp. 88, 89 and 90.

Allen, Hugh	Lieutenant	Augusta
Bracken, Matthew	Ensign	Botetourt
Bush, Michael	Private	Augusta
Cameron, George	-	Augusta
Croley, Samuel	Private	Botetourt
Cundiff, Jonathan	Ensign	Bedford
Fields, John	Colonel	Culpeper
Frogg, John	Lieutenant	Augusta
Hughey, Joseph	Private	Fincastle
Lewis, Charles	Colonel	Augusta
McClannahan, Robert	Captain	Botetourt
Moffett, William	Sergeant	Fincastle
Mooney, James	-	Fincastle
Murray, John	Captain	Botetourt
Stephen, William	-	Augusta
Ward, James	Captain	Botetourt
White, David	Private	Augusta
Williams, Thomas	Sergeant	Botetourt
Wilson, Samuel	Captain	Augusta[30]

Thus, we can see that eight of the nineteen listed as killed were from Augusta County. Since the militia soldiers engaged in the Battle at Point Pleasant were from many counties, James Lambert had contact with many soldiers outside of his own Militia District which included the counties of Augusta, Albemarle, Amherst and Buckingham

The following quotation on a company from Culpeper County gives us some further insight:

"On an August day in 1774, a company of forty men headed west from the county of Culpeper. They were on their way to join forces under Colonel Andrew Lewis who, by orders of Virginia's governor Dunmore, was preparing to march on Indian Nations, principally Shawnee, that were attacking along the frontier in the latest of sporadic uprisings.

At the head of the company was Colonel John Fields, a veteran of the French and Indian War and one of the most prestigious men in the county. Colonel Fields was born in Culpeper

---

30 Search Results for Dunmore's War, http://www.lva.lib.va.us/whatwehave/mil/vmd/ dunmore.asp, pp. 1-4 of 4, on 2/22/2008.

County in 1720. He married Anna Rogers Clark, sister of General George Rogers Clark. . . . After serving the legislature in 1765, he was made colonel of the militia . . . .

Along with Colonel Fields, were two of his son-in-laws, Lawrence and George Slaughter. In less than two years, George would find himself a captain and over a company of the Culpeper Minutemen . . . ."[31]

Colonel William Fleming wrote papers entitled: "An Extract from a Journal kept by An Officer in the Army under Col. Andw. Lewis on the expidition against Our Enemy Ohio Indians." He recorded that on October 8th Colonel Lewis was encamped at Point Pleasant with 800 men, "most of them Woodsmen well Armed, such as may be depended on." Further, that on the evening of October 9th a war party from the united tribes of Shawnee, Delaware, Mingoes, Taways and several other Nations crossed the Ohio river in over 70 rafts with a plan to attack the army camp by surprise. Some men left the army camp on the morning of October 10th. About three miles from the encampment, they were attacked by a large party of Indians just after day break. Not long after, the men were chased back into camp. The battle that followed was one of the fiercest ever fought between the colonists and the Eastern Indians. Colonel Fleming gives the best account of what happened by writing the following:

"Imagining this to be some scouting party, Col. Lewis ordered a detachment from every Company, so as to make up One hundred fifty men from each line, to go in quest of them." Colonel Lewis's brother, Charles, also a Colonel, led one of two detachments that marched out of camp. Fleming continues, "We Marched Briskly–3/4 of a mile or better from Camp, the Sun then, near an hour high, when a few guns were fired on the Right, succeeded by a heavy fire, which in an Instant extended to the left and the two lines were hotly engaged." Colonel Charles Lewis received a mortal wound at the start of the engagement, and was led off the field. Soon after, Colonel Fleming received a serious wound to the breast and arm and "Obleedged to quit the Field."[32]

It was now realized that the Indians had a greater force than was first thought. Reinforcements were ordered up from the camp. Colonel Fields raced to the front with reinforcements. He arrived just in time for the men there had just been pushed back 150 to 200 yards. With the aid of fresh troops, the ground was quickly regained and the enemy began to give ground.[33]

---

31 Culpeper in Lord Dunmore's War, http://www.liming.org/nwta/culdunmore.html , p. 1 of 4, on 2/21/2008.
32 Ibid., pp. 1 and 2 of 4, on 2/21/2008.
33 Ibid., p. 2.

Shortly after arriving on the scene, Colonel Fields was killed. According to Colonel William Preston, Fields was "shot at a great tree by two Indians on his Right while one on his left was amusing him with talk the Col. endeavouring to get a shot at him. Captain Shelby then took command of the wing.[34]

Colonel Fleming wrote further that "We had 7 or 800 Warriors to deal with. Never did Indians stick closer to it, nor behave bolder. The engagement lasted from half an hour after [sunrise], to the same time before Sunset. And let me add I believe the Indians never had such a Scourging for the English before, they scalpd many of their own dead to prevent their falling into Our hands, buried numbers, threw many into the Ohio and no doubt carried off many wounded. We found 70 Rafts, we took 18 Scalps, the most of them principle Warriors amongst the Shawnese camp."[35]

The army's losses varied according to different accounts; however, a figure that is considered accurate is around 75 killed and 150 wounded. Colonel Fleming reported that the Indian numbers were at least equal to the army's losses.[36]

Colonel Charles Lewis and His Augusta County Regiment

Charles Lewis was born on 11 March 1736 near present Staunton in Augusta County, Virginia. He was a prominent Virginia planter and a member of the Virginia House of Burgesses from 1773 to 1774. As a Colonel in the Virginia Militia, he led the forces of the Augusta County Regiment at Point Pleasant (which is now in West Virginia) during Lord Dunmore's War. On the morning of October 10, 1774, he led the attack of 150 officers and men, in the Battle of Point Pleasant, an engagement that pitted his Virginians against the famous Indian Chief Cornstalk and the Confederacy Indian Nations. Colonel Lewis was mortally wounded and died a short time later. He was buried with his fellow slain officers in the magazine on October 10, 1774. A large monument in the memory of Colonel Charles Lewis stands in the Tu Eudie Wie State Park in Point Pleasant, Mason County, West Virginia.[37]

"But few of the rolls of Companies which participated in the battle of Point Pleasant, or which arrived on the field that evening with Colonel William Christian, are known to be in existence. Far the greater number have been lost in the shades of oblivion. It is possible

---

34 Ibid.
35 Ibid., p. 3.
36 Ibid.
37 Charles Lewis (1736-1774) - Find A Grave Memorial, http://www.findagrave.com, p. 1 of 2, on 2/24/2008.

that some others, in addition to those we now have, may yet be found, among the musty and dusty documents of public record offices and libraries, but this is not probable. There were eleven companies in the Augusta Regiment, under Colonel Charles Lewis . . . ."[38]

". . . General (Andrew) Lewis rendezvoused at Lewisburg, Camp Union, about the 4th of September. His brother, Col. Charles Lewis had command of the Augusta Companies, under Captains George Matthews, Alexander McClenachan, John Dickenson, John Lewis, Benjamin Harrison, William Paul, Joseph Haynes and Samuel Wilson. Colonel William Fleming commanded the Botetourt companies, under Captains Matthew Arbuckle, John Murray, John Lewis, James Robertson, Robert McClenachan, James Ward, and John Stuart. Col. John Fields . . . raised a company in Culpeper, his native county, and joined the camp. Captains Evan Shelby, William Russell, and _____ Herbert, led companies from Washington: and Captain Thomas Buford, from Bedford. These four companies were to be under Col. William Christian, who was collecting more men, and expected to join Lewis at Point Pleasant. On the 11th of the month General Lewis began his march for the mouth of the Kenawha, his forces amounting to about eleven hundred men. There was no track for the army and few white men had ever gone down the Kenawha. Capt. Matthew Arbuckle was the principal pilot through the mountains. The army received its supplies from pack horses and droves of cattle that followed in the rear, and performed the march one hundred and sixty miles in 19 days . . . ."[39]

"A braver force was never raised in Virginia than that which marched to Point pleasant under Lewis. 'It consisted,' says Captain Stuart, 'chiefly of young volunteers, well trained to the use of arms, as hunting in those days was much practiced, and preferred to agricultural pursuits by enterprising young men. The produce of the soil was of little value on the west side of the Blue Ridge, the ways bad, and the distance to market too great to make it esteemed. Such pursuits enured them to hardships and dangers. They had no knowledge of the use of discipline or military order, when in an enemy's country, well skilled in their own manner of warfare, and were quite unacquainted with military operations of any kind. Ignorance of their duties, together with high notions of Independence and equality of condition, rendered the service extremely difficult and disagreeable to the commander, who was by nature of a lofty and high military spirit.' One of the Augusta companies that took its departure from Staunton excited admiration for the height and uniformity of their stature. In the bar room of Sampson Matthews' tavern a measure was taken. The greater part of the men in the company were six feet two inches without their shoes. But two were

38 Dunmore's War Rosters, http://www.accessgenealogy.com, p. 1 of 3, on 2/24/2008.
39 Shawnee Chief Cornstalk, http://victorian.fortunecity.com, p. 3 of 9, on 2/24/2008.

only six feet. This mark remained upon the wall till the tavern was consumed by fire in 1833."[40]

"Patriotic and brave the Valley boys submitted to the rigid discipline of Lewis with reluctance, but fought with valor. Passing through an untrod wilderness they outmarched Dunmore on a beaten track . . . ."[41]

The Archives of the Virginia State Library maintains on microfilm a list of Virginia soldiers in the Dunmore's War. A researcher discovered from Augusta County records that a court of claims was held on 17-19 January 1775 to settle the payroll claims of Captain Jonas Friend and his Company in the Augusta County Regiment at the Battle of Point Pleasant. The Company was gone from the Tygarts Valley for 48 days and 20 survivors from the company were listed. The rank and file were paid 1 shilling 6d a day and Indian scouts were paid 5 shillings daily for the extra risks they took. The survivors listed in the Jonas Friend Company who James Lambert mentioned in his Pension File documents included the following:

*"**Joseph Friend.** Paid three pounds and 12 shillings for 48 days, he was born about 1750, the eldest son of Captain Friend and his wife Sarah Skidmore and was later a Captain of Spies under Anthony Wayne. He died in what is now Webster County, West Virginia, in 1827.*

***Andrew Skidmore.** He was paid one pound 7 shillings for only 18 days. He was born on 8 November 1750 in Virginia. . . . He was wounded in the hand at Point Pleasant . . . . He died on 15 November 1827 in what is now Sutton in Braxton County.*

***James Stewart.** Paid three pounds 12 shillings for 48 days. He is said to have died before the death of John Stewart and his family . . . and nothing more is known of him.*

***John Stewart.** Paid three pounds 12 shillings for 48 days. He lived on Stewarts Run on the east side at the southern end of Tygarts River near the present town of Mingo, he, his wife and child, were killed on 16 December 1778 by Indians, and his sister-in-law, a certain Miss Hamilton, was taken prisoner. William Hamilton was appointed his administrator, and his estate was appraised on 28 March 1778 (9) by Benjamin Wilson and John Warrick..*

---

40 Ibid.
41 Ibid.

William White [Junior]. The best paid, he had 23 pounds 10 shillings from the public purse for 94 days as a scout. He was born on Cedar Creek in what is now Shenandoah County, Virginia, and was living in the Buckhannon Settlement by 1771. . . Captain White married Elizabeth Wallace (who was still living at the age of 102) and was killed by the Indians at Buckhannon Fort in 1782 . . ."[42]

David White, a brother of William White, is the only one of those killed at Point Pleasant who was definitely in Captain Friend's Company.[43]

It must be noted that James Lambert in 1844 was attempting at age 86 to recall the details of a period of three months and the specifics of a one day battle that occurred some 70 years previous when he was only 16 years old. It is remarkable to me that his recollections were so accurate as to the time, place, duration, events and results of the Battle at Point Pleasant. For example, he recalled that he volunteered for his first tour of duty of three months duration in the summer and fall of 1774; that he was marched between Wilson Station and the mouth of the Kanawha River, crossing the Cheat River, Laurel Fork and Glady Fork; that the one day Battle, starting shortly after sunrise and ending shortly before sunset, was at the mouth of the Kanawha River; that the Indians were defeated after a tough struggle, and that the Indians threw some of their dead warriors into the Ohio River.

James Lambert was also able to recall the names of some officers and certain events relative to the one day Battle. For example, he recalled that his Regiment from Augusta County was under the command of Colonel Charles Lewis and that he was killed in the Battle. He further recalled a Lieutenant or Captain John Frogg who commanded in the right wing at the Battle and that he was also killed in the engagement. Others he recalled included Captain Skidmore who was wounded in the Battle and a Lieutenant Colonel Rafe Stewart. James Lambert also stated his personal experience of having *"received several (musket) balls through his clothes."*[44]

Material on the Descendants of Richard Skidmore includes the following historical data relative to John A. Skidmore and his brother, Andrew Skidmore (a member of Jonas Friend's Company):

---

42 Captain Jonas Friend and his Company at Battle of Point Pleasant, http://www.swcp.com, pp. 2 and 4 of 11, on 2/24/2008.

43 Ibid., pp. 4 and 5.

44 See Appendix, Item 3, p. 124.

"John A. Skidmore, a son of Joseph and Agnes Ann (Caldwell) Skidmore, was born on the plantation 'Fisher's Delight' in Kent County, Delaware, June 10, 1736. Soon after his birth, the family moved to that part of Augusta County, Virginia, that is now Pendleton County, WV.

John served in the Augusta County Militia during the French and Indian War. He was called out in 1755 and served until the end of the War. John married Mary Magalena Hinkle in the early 1760's. Mary was a daughter of John Justus and Magdalena (Eschemann) Hinkle. John Hinkle and his family settled in the section of Virginia known as Germany Valley and were the builders of Hinkle's fort.

In 1767, John Skidmore was appointed Captain of the Augusta Militia and in 1770, he was commissioned as one of His Majesty's Justices for Augusta County. In 1774, John's company of the Augusta Militia was mobilized for service in Dunmore's War and took part in the battle of Point Pleasant. John was wounded twice during the battle of Point Pleasant, in the leg and in the hip.

In 1778, John was appointed a justice of the newly formed Rockingham County by Patrick Henry. The first Rockingham County Court, in session April 28, 1778, found John A. Skidmore 'fit to serve as major' of the Augusta Militia. John declined the appointment but retained his captaincy for several years.

When Pendleton County was formed in 1778, John was elected the first president of the new court. John served the new County several years, including two terms as sheriff. John died in Pendleton County October 12, 1809 and Mary died October 18, 1829. . . .

Andrew Skidmore, a son of Joseph and Agnes Ann (Caldwell) Skidmore, was born in Augusta County, Virginia, November 11, 1750 and died in Braxton County, VA (WV) November 15, 1827. Andrew served in the VA Militia in Lord Dunmore's War and had a finger shot off at the Battle of Point Pleasant. He also served the Colonies in the American Revolution.

He married Margaret Johnson. Margaret, a daughter of Arthur and Margaret (Phares) Johnson, was born in Augusta County, VA in May 1759 and died in Randolph County VA in 1708 (1808)."[45]

---

45 Descendants of Richard Skidmore, http://www.rootsweb.com/~hcpd/norman/ SKIDMORE.htm, pp. 4 and 5 of 32, on 2/20/2008.

Material on the James Stewart Family who came to Augusta County, Virginia, from Ireland reads as follows:

". . . James Stewart . . . and Mary Ann Stewart had at least four sons, namely: Robert b. 1740-1743; James b. ca. 1744; Ralph b. 1747; and John b. ca. 1748. . . . The first record of James Stewart in Augusta County was March 18, 1747/48 when the county Court ordered him and others to build a road from the Lower Cowpasture River to Carter's Mill on the Cowpasture River. . . .

In 1755, James Stewart was a Captain in the Augusta Militia under John Dickinson. He and his son, James, Jr., were captured in 1757 by Shawnee Indians. James' son John witnessed the attack, but was able to escape to the fort. James was burned at the stake in front of his son, James, Jr., who later escaped or was released. . . .

Three of James' sons were classified by the courts as infants, and on February 17, 1762, in Orphans Court of Augusta County, eighteen-year old James Stuart (Stewart), Jr., orphan of James Stewart, was bound out to John Hamilton (husband of Mary, James' sister) as his guardian, his fifteen year old brother, Ralph Stewart, chose his older brother Robert Stewart as his guardian, and his fourteen year old brother, John Stewart, chose Henry Murray as his guardian. . . .

Ralph Stewart was commissioned Captain in 1773 by Lord Dunmarra, Governor of Virginia. He served as a ranger at Point Pleasant under General Lewis in the battle of 1774. He qualified as Captain of the Virginia Militia in January of 1775. His commission was renewed in 1778 by Patrick Henry, then Governor of Virginia, and served under General Green in South Carolina, fought at Guilford Court House, Hot Water, Ground Squirrel Ridge, Charlottesville and Yorktown where he was wounded in the right arm by a saber cut from Butcher Tarleton."[46]

An additional write-up on Captain Ralph Stewart reads as follows:

"Born in Augusta County, Virginia, 1752, later removed to Giles and Montgomery County, and died in Logan County, November 17, 1835. . . .

Was commissioned captain in 1773 by Lord Dunmore, Governor of Virginia, and served as a ranger. Was at Point Pleasant under General Lewis in the battle in 1774. In 1778, his commission was renewed by Patrick Henry, then Governor of Virginia, was ordered

---

46 James Stewart b. abt 1719, Northern Ireland, d. 09 Sep 1757, Augusta, Bath County, Virg. . ., http://www.stewartdna.org/10016-n.shtml, pp. 1 and 2 of 3, on 2/15/2008.

with his company to South Carolina to join the army under General Green, and was attached to a regiment commanded by Colonel Robert McCleary and Major Smith. Fought at Guilford Courthouse, Hot Water, Ground Squirrel, Charlottesville, and Yorktown. He was wounded in the right arm by a sabre cut from one of 'Butcher' Tarleton's men and was on the invalid roll for the state of Virginia. His commission and discharge, left with Colonel George Pearis for safe-keeping, were lost or stolen when the latter's home was plundered.

Soldier received pension in 1834 and his widow received pension in 1846 at which time she was 74 years old. . . ."[47]

It is my belief that the Ralph Stewart mentioned above is the Lieut. Col. Rafe Stewart James Lambert referenced on the first page of his Amended Declaration (13 May 1844).

You will recall that the guardian appointed in 1762 for James Stewart, Jr. was his brother-in-law, John Hamilton, and the administrator appointed after the deaths of the James Stewart Jr.'s family on 16 December 1778 was another brother-in-law, William Hamilton. Therefore, it is clear that the Stewart and Hamilton families of Augusta County had very close relationships.

The Hamilton family, also originally from Ireland, came to Augusta County in the 1740s, and the following quotation gives us a further understanding about them:

"Major Andrew Hamilton was born in Augusta County in 1741. His parents were Archibald and Frances Calhoun Hamilton . . . (and they had) five sons, Audley, John, Andrew, William, and Archibald, and a daughter, named Lettice. Andrew Hamilton married . . . Jane Magill, a native of Pennsylvania, and in 1765 removed to South Carolina and settled in Abbeville, in the neighborhood of Andrew Pickens, afterwards the celebrated General Pickens, who had gone with his parents from Augusta some years previously. Both Hamilton and Pickens entered the military service at the beginning of the Revolutionary war. The former served through the whole war, first as captain and then as major under General Pickens, and took part in nearly all the important battles in South Carolina and Georgia . . . The life of Major Hamilton was long and eventful. He died January 19, 1835, in the ninety-fifth year of his age, his wife having died April 20, 1826, in her eighty-sixth year. The remains of this aged and distinguished couple lie in the cemetery of Upper Long Cane Church, of which General Pickens and Major Hamilton are said to have been the first elders. . . .

---

47 Johnston, Ross B., <u>West Virginians in the American Revolution</u>, http://www.ancestry.com,
    p. 274, on 2/15/2008.

Major Hamilton and one of his daughters, Mrs. Alston, made a trip on horseback from South Carolina to Augusta county, to visit the spot where he was born and reared. It was his first visit—one of tender remembrance—since he left the county in his youth. A brother of his went to Kentucky, and was the founder of a wealthy and distinguished family."[48]

It is possible that the references to Major Hamilton in the Amended Declaration of James Lambert (13 May 1844) were to this Major Andrew Hamilton, since he was a native of Augusta County, Virginia. There were many members of the Hamilton family in Augusta County and this Major Hamilton may have been known by the nick name of "Guy".

Although it has been reported that Major Andrew Hamilton moved with his family to South Carolina in the mid 1760s and only returned with his daughter to Augusta County at a later date to visit where he was born and raised, I have found some evidence that he was familiar with Point Pleasant and may have been in the area on other occasions.

It has been reported that in the summer of 1777 three or four companies were raised in Botetourt and Augusta counties which were under the command of Colonel George Shilleran. The chief officers in Greenbrier agreed to raise additional troops and cast lots who should command the new Company. The lot fell on Andrew Hamilton for Captain, and William Renick for Lieutenant. About forty men were collected and they joined Colonel Shilleran's party on their way to Point Pleasant.[49]

Although James Lambert referenced some soldiers who were in the Jonas Friend Company, I think it is most likely that James Lambert was a member in the Company of Captain John Skidmore. James Lambert listed Captain Skidmore immediately after he listed Colonel (Charles) Lewis and Major (Andrew or Guy) Hamilton in the second paragraph of his Amended Declaration (13 May 1844). No payroll record is known for Captain Skidmore's Company. Since Captain Skidmore was wounded at Point Pleasant, one can speculate that he was not physically able to file payroll claims

---

48 <u>Waddell's Annals of Augusta County, Virginia, from 1726 to 1871</u> - Chapter 3: From the First Court to the First Indian War - pp. 91 and 92, http://www.roanetnhistory.org, pp. 1-3, on 2/24/2008.

49 Revolutionary War - Primary Documents, Death of Cornstalk, Narrative by Captain John Stuart of General Andrew Lewis' Expedition Against the Indians in the Year 1774, and of the Battle of Pleasant Point, Virginia, in Magazine of American History, November 1877, http://www.wvculture.org, p. 1 of 3 on 2/24/2008.

for himself and his Company members and was not able to make an appearance at the Augusta County court of claims in January 1775.

James Lambert made references in his Amended Declaration (13 May 1844) to an Ensign William White. A Captain William White, Jr., was a member of Jonas Friend's Company. Captain William White and his brother, Lieutenant John White, are listed under West Virginians in the Revolution and their summaries read as follows:

John and William White were among the early settlers of Randolph County, Virginia, their settlement dating from 1772 to 1774. They were active in early Indian hostilities.

John, who held the rank of lieutenant, was killed by Indians from ambush in 1778.

Captain William White was first mentioned in Kercheval's History of the Valley of Virginia *when in 1734 he left Maryland and settled in Shenandoah County. As early as 1768, he was known as 'Captain White', and was led into Upshur County, by Samuel Pringle, where he became a guardian of the Buckhannon colony. With Colonels William Lowther, Jesse Hughes, and John Cutright, he was active at Bush's Fort on the Buckhannon River, West's Fort on Hacker's Creek, and Nutter's Fort at Clarksburg. He was captured by the Indians in 1778 but escaped. On March 15, 1782, he was killed by an Indian just across the river from the fort at Buckhannon and is buried in Heavner Cemetery, Upshur County. He is said to have been killed by a Delaware chief whose son White had killed some years before.*"[50]

It is clear that this is the William White that James Lambert recalled some 70 years later in connection with the Battle at Point Pleasant against the Indians in 1774.

One can imagine the anxiety of the families back home in Augusta and other Virginia counties, awaiting news of the outcome of the engagement with the Indian Nations. They were much aroused by the story of a child who awoke from sleep three times on October 10, screaming that the Indians were killing her father.[51]

"It was later discovered that the child's father, John Frogge, was among those killed at Point Pleasant."[52]

---

50 Johnston, Ross B., West Virginians in the American Revolution, http://www.ancestry.com, pp. 302 and 303, on 2/15/2008.
51 Colonel William Fleming in Dunmore's War, 1774, http://www.wvculture.org, p. 7 of 13, on 2/24/2008.
52 Ibid., footnote 61, p. 12 of 13.

Having stated his personal recollections in such detail and recalling the names of at least seven places and eight soldiers, a reasonable person could only conclude that James Lambert was in fact a participant at the Battle of Point Pleasant on October 10, 1774.

This was an important battle recognized by the United States Congress in 1908 as the first Battle of the American Revolution and cited by some historians as the most desperate struggle ever waged between white men and Indians in American.

After returning from the Battle of Point Pleasant, James Lambert moved with his father from Wilson Station and settled on the North Fork (South Branch) of the Potomac River in Augusta County, Virginia. (This location is now in Pendleton County, West Virginia). James Lambert continued to make his father's house at this location his home until after the close of the Revolutionary War in 1783.

The following information describes this location in greater detail:

"The North Fork South Branch Potomac River forms just north of the Virginia/West Virginia border in Pendleton County at the confluence of the Laurel Fork and Straight Fork along Big Mountain (3,881 feet). From Circleville, the North Fork flows northeast through Pendleton County between the Fore Knobs (2,949 feet) to its west and the River Knobs (2,490 feet) to its east . . . ."[53]

---

53 Potomac River - Wikipedia, the free encyclopedia, http://en.wikipedia.org, p. 7 of 10, on 11/22/2006.

Second Military Tour of Duty
Drafted for Three Months in 1775 at Age 17
No Battle

James Lambert stated in his Amended Declaration (13 May 1844) that his second military tour of duty started in July 1775 when he was drafted as a militiaman for the term of three months under the command of Colonel Hillyard, Captain Spencer, 1st Sergeant Hilldepeny and Corporal John . . . . He marched from the North Fork of the Potomac in Rockingham (Augusta) County to the Shenandoah in Loudon (Loudoun) County. There he remained for about ten days until more troops were collected from Greenbrier and Jackson River. The troops arrived under the command of Colonel Johnson and they took up their line of march for Richmond from Loudon (Loudoun) County. James Lambert marched to Page (County) at Swift Run Gap, thence to New Castle (only town now in Craig County) and thence to Richmond where he remained for one month. Then he marched to Manchester/Rocky Ridge (south side of the James River near Richmond) where he remained about one month until he returned home to Rockingham (Augusta) County. He served a full three months, being discharged in October 1775 by Captain Spencer.

James Lambert's second military tour of duty was apparently within Virginia and he was not engaged in any battle during these three months of 1775. However, he recalled the names of at least twelve places he visited and he mentioned the names of five soldiers in his militia unit.

The two battles of the American Revolution in 1775 were in Massachusetts against the British at Lexington and Concord on 19 April 1775 and Bunker Hill (Breed's Hill) on 17 June 1775. George Washington assumed command of the Continental Army on 3 July 1775.[54]

Fort Henckel Militia Muster Rolls June and September 1775

Fort Henckel, also known as, Hinkle's Fort, was located deep in the Allegheny Mountains in West Augusta County, Virginia. It was built in 1761-1762 by Johann

---

54 The World Book Encyclopedia (Field Enterprises Educational Corporation), Chicago, 1977, Q-R Volume 16, Revolutionary War, p. 260.

Justus Henckel (Hinkle) Sr. (1706-1778), and other members of his family with perhaps help from neighboring settlers. The location is near Riverton, Pendleton County, West Virginia, in what is known as the Germany Valley. The fort was built for the protection of the Henckel family and other pioneers against the Native Americans who frequented the valley from time to time. The fort was the only outpost in Pendleton County for the patriot forces during the American Revolutionary War. It was generally known that Henckel, Sr. served as commander of the fort and furnished supplies to the troops of the Virginia Militia who were quartered there. There has been no solid primary proof of his service and that of the Virginia Militia who were headquartered there, including the North Fork Military Company, which had been organized by settlers early in the Revolutionary War.[55]

From time to time, old records do turn up. Recently, Stephanie Mitchell, a researcher from the Midwest and a descendant of the Hinkle, Teter, Vandeventer, Cassel, Lambert, Bible and other Pendleton County, West Virginia families, unearthed two old records in a 1672 Bible of another of her ancestors, Joseph Louis Cheuvront (b. France 1757, d. Harrison County, now West Virginia, 1832). This well preserved Bible contains the Militia Muster Rolls for John Skidmore's Company at Fort Henckel (modern spelling Hinkle) for June 6 and September 8, 1775.[56]

The best part of this recent find is the recognition these listings give to forty-nine men for their service to our fledgling nation. Of course, the proof these musters provide to the descendants of these men for eligibility in organizations such as DAR and SAR is also important. Copies of these pages are now a part of the holdings of the National Society, Daughters of the American Revolution.[57]

The Muster Roll for 6 June 1775 listed the following:

> Johann Justus Henckel, Commander of Fort and 6 June 1775 Militia
> Capt. John Skidmore Company
> Johann Justus Henckel, Jr.
> Moses Elsworth
> Jacob Henckel
> Adam Biewel

---

55 Fort Henckel Militia Muster Rolls, http://www.hackerscreek.com/forthenckelmilitia1775. htm, p. 1 of 2, on 5/5/2008.

56 Ibid.

57 Ibid.

Paul Teeter
George Teeter
Phillip Teeter
Andrew Johnston
Abraham Henckel
Isaac Henckel
Paul Henckel
Moses Henckel
Joseph Skidmore
Martin Peterson
James Cunningham
Wm. Cunningham
Christian Strely
Joseph Cheuvront
Valentino Felty Castle
Peter Challe
Jacob Challe
Joseph Bennett
John Bennett
Wm. Bennett
Johann Biewel
Wm. Gregg
Jacob Rule
Joseph Rule
Robert Mennes
Godfrey Bumgardner
John Phearis
Thomas Miller
Michel Miller
George Miller
Dan House
Jacob House
Matthias House
George Dunkel
Jon Dunkel
Zach Weese
Jon Weese
Jacob Weese

Jon Lambert
Arthur Johnston
John Smith
Daniel Little
Alex Robbins[58]

The Muster Roll for 8 September 1775 listed the same 49 soldiers; however, the name Andrew Johnston appears twice and the second entry should have been Arthur Johnston, and the spelling of the first name of John Smith was changed to Jon.[59]

Since James Lambert has told us he served in the Virginia militia from July to October 1775, it was my first thought that he might be the soldier referenced as "Jon Lambert" in the Musters Rolls for 6 June and 8 September 1775. Since John Lambert was the father of James Lambert, perhaps the given name of Jon was just entered in error. However, it is not likely that such an error would be made on both Muster Rolls. In addition, James named different officers for his 2nd tour of duty, such as, Colonel Hillyard and Captain Spencer, Therefore, I have concluded that James Lambert was a member of another militia unit at that time.

However, I think it is quite likely that the Jon Lambert listed in both Muster Rolls was in fact John Lambert, the father of James Lambert. John Lambert was approximately 40 years of age at the time and many of his neighbors were included in both Muster Rolls; namely, Moses Elsworth, George Teeter, Phillip Teeter, Andrew Johnston, Isaac Henckel, James Cunningham, and Joseph Bennett.[60]

58 General Muster of Joseph Louis Cheuvront, 6 June 1775 Militia, http://www.hackerscreek.com, pp. 1 and 2 of 2, on 5/5/2008.

59 General Muster of Fort Henckel, 8 September 1775 Militia, http://www/hackerscreek.com, pp. 1 and 2 of 2, on 5/5/2008.

60 Census-Henkle, Rockingham County, Virginia, Heads of Families at the First Census of the United States 1784, p. 7, http://www.rootsweb.com, pp. 1 and 2 of 2, on 5/9/2007.

THIRD MILITARY TOUR OF DUTY
SUBSTITUTE FOR JACOB ELLSWORTH FOR SIX MONTHS IN 1775/76 AT AGES 17/18
BATTLE OF GREAT BRIDGE ON 9 DECEMBER 1775

James Lambert stated in his Amended Declaration (13 May 1844) that his third tour of duty started in November 1775, one month after his discharge from his second tour of duty in October 1775. He further stated that his third tour of duty was for the period of six months as a substitute for Jacob Ellsworth.[61]

Jacob Ellsworth

Claims for supplies given for military use in the Dunmarra War of 1774 were certified in a Court of Augusta on 18 August 1775. One of the citizens who made such a claim was Moses Ellsworth.[62]

The original copies of the first census in 1790 for Virginia were burned during the War of 1812. In an effort to reconstruct the census, manuscript lists of state enumerations for the years 1782 through 1785 were compiled.[63] The 1784 Census for Rockingham County, Virginia, contained a List of Isaac Henkle, being Page 7, which included forty of his neighbors, such as, John Lambert, Andw Johnston (Andrew Johnson), Moses Elsworth, Sr., Moses Elsworth, Jr., and Joseph Bennett.[64] Thus, there were Elsworth or Ellsworth families living in the area where James Lambert also lived with his father, John Lambert, and undoubtedly Jacob Ellsworth was a member of an Elsworth or Ellsworth family in that neighborhood.

---

61 See Appendix, Item 3, p. 124.

62 Morton, Oren F., <u>A History of Pendleton County, West Virginia</u>, Reprinted for Clearfield Company Inc. by Genealogical Publishing Co. Inc., Baltimore, MD, 1990, Section III, Military, Supplies for Military Use, p. 393.

63 Census - Rorok, Rockingham County, Virginia, Heads of Families at the First Census of the United States 1784, p. 1, http://www.rootsweb.com/~varockin/censusmr.htm, p. 1 of 4, on 5/9/2007.

64 Census - Henkle, Rockingham County, Virginia, Heads of Families at the First Census of the United States 1784, p. 7, http://www.rootsweb.com/~varockin/censusih.htm., p. 1 of 2, on 5/9/2007.

Jacob Ellsworth is considered a Patriot of the American Revolutionary War by the National Society of the Sons of the American Revolution. The Family Group Records for Jacob Ellsworth show that he was born in Rowan County, North Carolina in 1750, and that his parents were Moses Ellsworth, also a Patriot, and Anna Maria Elizabeth Henckel. The wife of Jacob Ellsworth was Hannah and they were married about 1770 in Augusta County, Virginia. Their children included John Ellsworth, who was born in 1771 in Augusta County, Virginia, married Susannah Bumgarner on 28 Jun 1792 in Harrison County, West Virginia, and died before 1831 in Madison County, Indiana. Their other son was Jacob Ellsworth, Jr., who married Rachael Bibby. Their daughter was Mary Ellsworth, who married Jacob Collins. **Jacob Ellsworth served as a Private in the Virginia Militia.** He died in 1825/1826 in Clark County, Ohio, and his wife, Hannah, died at the same location after 1819.[65]

Augusta County Militia

James Lambert was a resident of Augusta County at the time of the following legislative action in 1775:

"The Virginia Colony Convention, which managed the affairs of Virginia from the time the old system of government disappeared until the adoption of the first Constitution of the State in 1776, passed an ordinance on July 17, 1775, for raising two regiments of regulars, and for organizing the militia. The first regiment was to consist of 544 rank and file with a colonel, lieutenant-colonel, major, 8 captains, 16 lieutenants, and 8 ensigns, and the second of 476 rank and file, with seven companies and corresponding officers. The field officers were appointed by the Convention; namely, Patrick Henry to command the first regiment, William Woodford the second. The companies were to consist of 68 men each, to be enlisted in districts, and to serve one year. The companies raised in the district composing Augusta etc., to be 'expert riflemen.' The company officers were appointed by the members of the Convention from the district.

The whole State was divided into military districts, and the militia were ordered to be embodied as minute-men. The counties of Buckingham, Amherst, Albemarle and Augusta constituted one district. Each district was to raise a battalion of 500 men, rank and file, from the age of 16 to that of 50, to be divided into ten companies of 50 men each. The officers were to be appointed by committees selected by the various county committees. The battalion was required to be kept in training at some convenient place for twelve days, twice

---

65 National Society of the Sons of the American Revolution, SAR Patriot Index Edition III Database, Copyright 1995-2002.

a year, and several companies to be mustered four days in each month, except December, January and February, in their respective counties.

Every man so enlisted was required to 'furnish himself with a good rifle, if to be had, otherwise with a tomahawk, common firelock, bayonet, pouch, or cartouch box, and three charges of powder and ball. Upon affidavit that the minuteman was not able to furnish his arms, etc., they were to be supplied at public expense. The officers were required to equip themselves, and officers and men were liable to a fine for failure in this respect.

For the only account of any proceedings under the ordinances passed by the State Convention in July 1775, providing for the organization of 'minute men,' we are indebted to the 'Gilmer Papers,' issued in 1887 by the Virginia Historical Society.

Colonel Woodford was born in Caroline county; served in the French and Indian wars, commanded at the battle of Great Bridge, December 9, 1775; was promoted to Brig. General and participated in various battles; wounded at Brandywine; made prisoner in 1780, at siege of Charleston; taken to New York, and died there, Nov. 13, 1780, aged 45."[66]

"Commissioners from the counties of Buckingham, Amherst, Albemarle and Augusta, composing a district, met on 8th of September, 1775, at the house of James Woods, in Amherst, now Nelson. The commissioners from Augusta were Sampson Mathews, Alexander McClanahan and Samuel McDowell. It was resolved that Augusta furnish four companies of fifty men each, and that each of the other counties furnish two companies, making a total of ten companies and five hundred men required by the ordinance. George Mathews, of Augusta, was chosen colonel; Charles Lewis of Albemarle, lieutenant-colonel; David Gaines, major; and Thomas Patterson (or Patteson, doubtless, of Buckingham), 'commissary of masters.'

The officers appointed for the Augusta companies were as follows:

1st Benjamin Harrison, captain; Henry Evans, lieutenant, and Curord Custard, ensign.

2nd Daniel Stephenson, captain, John McMahon, lieutenant, and Samuel Henderson, ensign.

3rd Alexander Long, captain, James Sayres, lieutenant, and John Buchanan, ensign.

---

66 Waddell's Annals of Augusta County, Virginia, from 1726 to 1871, Chapter 9: The War of the Revolution, etc. from 1775 to 1779, p. 244, http://www.roanetnhistory.org, pp. 1 and 2 of 2, on 2/15/2008.

4ᵗʰ William Lyle, Jr., lieutenant, and William Moore, ensign. The captain of this company was not named.

The first company was evidently intended to be raised in the northern part of the county, now Rockingham, and the fourth in the southern part, now Rockbridge.

The regiment was required to meet on the east side of the Blue Ridge, at a point to be designated by the colonel, within three miles of Rockfish Gap.

As far as we have learned, no other proceedings were taken in pursuance of the ordinance, and probably the regiment never mustered. In December following, an ordinance was passed for raising seven regiments of regulars, in addition to the First and Second, and George Mathews was then appointed by the Convention lieutenant-colonel of the Ninth. The latter ordinance superseded the former, which proposed merely a militia organization.

The ordinance of July, 1775, also called for two regiments of regulars, the First and Second, and the district commissioners, at their meeting in September, designated the officers for two companies. Among them was Thomas Hughes, but whether captain or lieutenant it is impossible to tell from Dr. Gilmer's memorandum. William Robertson, of Augusta, was chosen a lieutenant.

Lieutenant Robertson entered the service in 1775, and was at the battles of Great Bridge, Bandywine and Germantown. Being a member of Colonel Mathews' regiment at Germantown, he was taken prisoner there, and detained three years. After his discharge, he rejoined the army and served till the close of the war. He died November 12, 1831."[67]

Third Tour Locations

James Lambert stated in his Amended Declaration (13 May 1844) that his third tour of duty included the following locations; namely, Rockingham (Augusta), New Castle, Richmond, Manchester, another town on the James River twenty to thirty miles from Richmond, and finally Norfolk.[68]

Rockingham County was not created from Augusta County until 1778.[69]

New Castle is the county seat of Craig County[70] and is located north west of Roanoke.

---

67 Ibid., pp. 244-246.

68 See Appendix, Item 3, p. 125.

69 Rockingham County, Virginia - Wikipedia, the free encyclopedia, http://en.wikipedia.org/wiki/Rockingham_County_Virginia, p. 1 of 3, on 2/20/2008.

70 New Castle, Virginia - Wikipedia, the free encyclopedia, http://en.wikipedia.org/wiki/New_Castle_Virginia, p. 1 of 2, on 2/20/2008.

Manchester, Virginia, was the original county seat of Chesterfield County, Virginia, when it was formed from Henrico County in 1749. Originally known as Rocky Ridge, it was located on the south bank of the James River opposite Richmond on the north side of the river. Manchester became an incorporated town in 1769. In modern times, "Old Manchester" is considered a neighborhood of Richmond.[71]

Norfolk, Virginia, is located in the Hampton Roads region, named for the large natural harbor of the same name located at the mouth of Chesapeake Bay. The city is bordered to the west by the Elizabeth River and to the north by the Chesapeake Bay. It also shares land borders with the independent cities of Chesapeake to its south and Virginia Beach to its east.[72]

Great Bridge, Virginia, is a community located today in the independent city of Chesapeake and its name is derived from the American Revolutionary War Battle of Great Bridge, which took place on December 9, 1775 and resulted in the final removal of British government from the Colony and Dominion of Virginia.[73]

There is a map which was drawn in 1781 and it depicts the area at the mouth of the James River at Hampton Roads, Virginia.[74]

King's Bridge or Great Bridge?

James Lambert also stated that:

"Applicant (James Lambert) may also be mistaken as to the precise year when this tour was rendered, but it was the same year that the engagement called the Scrimmage of the King's Bridge. He was in that engagement and it was in his three months tour before his Six months tour as a substitute for Ellsworth or in this Six months tour and the department

---

71 Manchester, Virginia - Wikipedia, the free encyclopedia, http://en.wikipedia.org/wiki/Manchester_Virginia, p. 1 of 3, on 2/20/2008.

72 Norfolk, Virginia - Wikipedia, the free encyclopedia, http://en.wikipedia.org/wiki/Norfolk,_Vriginia, pp. 1 and 2 of 21, on 2/20/2008.

73 Great Bridge, Virginia - Wiikipedia, the free encyclopedia, http://en.wikipedia.org/wiki/Great_Bridge,_Virginia, p. 1 of 2, on 2/12/2008.

74 Mouth of James River Map, West Virginia, Southern Campaigns of the American Revolution, Vol. 4, No. 1, January - March 2007, Battle of Great Bridge by David K. Wilson, http://www.lib.jrshelby.com/scar.htm,, p. 41, on 3/29/2008.

must decide the year from that fact. At all events he served his tour of Six months, and was discharged in writing by Col. Hillyard."[75]

As you can tell, James Lambert was not sure of the precise year his third military tour of duty commenced.

James Lambert said that he was in the engagement called the Scrimmage of the King's Bridge and he left it up to the War Department to decide the time of his third tour from that event.

My research indicates that the King's Bridge engagement occurred on Saturday, November 16, 1776. Four thousand Hessians came down from the north over King's Bridge, which was a wooden bridge over the Harlem River, connecting Manhattan Island, then known as York Island, to the mainland of New York. By ten o'clock the British General Howe had committed 8,000 troops to the assault, nearly four times the number of those defending Fort Washington. The farthest reach of the Fort's outer defense was about five miles, north and south, and the Hessians faced the steepest, roughest terrain and withering fire from Virginia and Maryland riflemen positioned among the rocks under Colonel Moses Rawlings.[76]

Although King's Bridge is not referenced separately in a listing of major American Revolution battles, one highlight of the Revolutionary War was the capture of Fort Washington by the British on 16 November 1776.[77]

Since James Lambert did not set forth any personal observations of his experiences in the King's Bridge engagement and he made no reference that he was under the command of Moses Rawlings and Otho Williams, I began to question whether James Lambert was one of the 250 riflemen under their command. Further, James Lambert had said in his Amended Declaration (13 May 1844) that:

"He was marched to Richmond and served for three months when he was discharged in October 1775 by Capt. Spencer. He remained at home one month when he entered the service a third time. He entered as a substitute for six months for one Jacob Ellsworth."[78]

---

75 See Appendix, Item 3, p. 124.

76 McCullough, David, <u>1776</u>, (Simon & Schuster, New York, 2005), pp. 122, 240 and 241.

77 <u>The World Book Encyclopedia</u> (Field Enterprises Educational Corporation), Chicago, 1977, Q-R Volume 16, pp. 260 and 265.

78 See Appendix, Item 3, p. 124.

I also noted that James Lambert made no reference to New York with respect to his third military tour of duty; however, he said the following with respect to his fourth tour of duty:

4ᵗʰ Tour. He marched to Richmond, was quartered in the Capitol, stayed there for about three months, was engaged in frequent Scouts, took shipping at Rockets Landing two miles from Richmond and went to Norfolk stayed there several weeks cannot say how long- from thence he went to West Point on the North river, quartered there the winter of 1780 (the cold winter) and was engaged in building Block Houses."[79]

Although James Lambert was actually accurate with respect to the time frame of his third tour of duty, I have concluded that his reference to King's Bridge was actually a reference to Great Bridge.

It is my analysis of the Amended Declaration of James Lambert (13 May 1844) that James Lambert commenced his third military tour of six months in November 1775 as a substitute for Jacob Ellsworth. This tour included marches from Rockingham (Augusta) to the following locations within Virginia: New Castle, Richmond, Manchester, another unnamed town some 20-30 miles down the James River, and then to Norfolk. He was discharged by Colonel Crawford probably in the month of April 1776.

Therefore, it is my opinion, that James Lambert was engaged in the Battle of Great Bridge, Virginia, on the 9ᵗʰ day of December 1775.

In the 1700s, the village of Great Bridge was a center for transporting products from the forests and fields south of Chesapeake Bay and it was located on the Southern Branch of the Elizabeth River in Virginia's Norfolk County not far from the North Carolina border…The Great Road was little more than a dirt trail.[80]

In 1775, the crossing over the Southern Branch of the Elizabeth River was a forty foot span bridge through marsh land. It is important to note that the Albemarle and Chesapeake Canal did not come into existence until the 1850s.[81]

---

79 Ibid., p. 126.
80 Wingo, Elizabeth B. and Hanbury, Elizabeth B., The Battle of Great Bridge, The Norfolk County Historical Society of Chesapeake, Virginia, and The Chesapeake Public Schools, March, 1998, p. 1.
81 Ibid., p. 2.

Virginia's General Assembly adjourned 24 June 1775 without passing a single piece of legislation, since the entire session had been spent arguing with Lord Dunmore, the Royal Governor of Virginia. In August 1775, a Committee of Safety was created to govern the Virginia Colony and Edmund Pendleton was elected chairman. On 18 September 1775, the Committee of Safety made the decision to raise two regiments in the Colony. Colonel Patrick Henry was made the commander of the First Regiment and Colonel William Woodford was made the commander of the Second Regiment.[82]

"Inspired by his victory in the skirmish at Kempsville, Dunmore determined to attack Colonel Woodford at Great Bridge. . . . Thus the stage was set for the first land battle of the American Revolution in Virginia."[83]

The American and British forces both recognized the strategic location of the Great Bridge and both sides desired to control it. The British knew they could not survive in water-bound Norfolk or on their ships in the harbor without the supplies that came over the Great Bridge. The American Patriots wanted to break the supply line to the British.[84]

"Colonel William Woodford and the main body of his troops marched to Great Bridge, arriving there the second day of December (1775). . . .

Woodford's Second Virginia Regiment included the Minutemen of Culpepper County, 100 men from Fauquier County, and 100 from Orange County. The Minutemen marched under the famous Culpepper banner whose yellow ground bore the coiled rattlesnake and the words 'Don't Tread on Me - Liberty or Death.' The Minutemen were also called 'shirtmen' because, in lieu of uniforms, they wore hunting shirts and for headgear, either a hat with a buck tail or a coonskin cap with a dangling coon's tail. Home-made leather breeches and moccasins completed a costume as comfortable as it was picturesque. On many shirts the words of Patrick Henry, 'Liberty or Death' were displayed in white letters. These men, famed for their excellent marksmanship were a grim and determined lot."[85]

The night before the battle it was estimated that the men of the Virginia Second Regiment, the Culpepper Minutemen, and the militia from various localities numbered about one thousand.[86]

---

82 Ibid., pp. 5 and 6.
83 Ibid., p. 8.
84 Ibid., p. 9.
85 Ibid., p. 11.
86 Ibid., p. 14.

"A father and son from Fauquier County were among the officers serving with the Patriot forces. Major Thomas Marshall was one of those who helped organize the soldiers from Orange, Culpepper and Fauquier Counties into the elite regiment known as the Culpepper Minutemen. His eldest son, John, who later became Chief Justice of the Supreme Court of the United States, was a lieutenant in one of the companies. Major Marshall is credited with arranging the inducement for the British to attack. His well-coached servant 'deserted' to the enemy's side. The servant informed the British that there were only 300 shirtmen in the village of Great Bridge, but that several hundred more were expected the next day from North Carolina and that they would be bringing artillery."[87]

The Battle of Great Bridge, Virginia, on 9 December 1775

At dawn of 9 December 1775, Captain Leslie, who commanded the British regulars, ordered the gunners from the ship *Otter* to open fire and started his infantry toward the bridge. The British quickly replaced planks they had removed from the bridge, and Captain Charles Fordyce called his company of grenadiers into formation. While the two canon at the British Fort Murray poured grapeshot into the breastworks of the Patriots, Fordyce and his men moved forward on the Great Bridge, six abreast smartly attired in their redcoats with bayonets fixed.[88]

The Virginians were ordered to withhold their fire until the British were only 50 yards away. When the Virginians fired, the British staggered, stopped, and then fell back. Captain Fordyce rallied his troops and they began to move forward again; however, another volley from the Virginians killed Captain Fordyce and two of his Lieutenants. More reinforcements joined the Patriots who were firing from the breastworks. The fire was too heavy for the exposed British and those who were not killed or severely wounded turned and retreated on the bridge in great haste. Colonel Edward Stephens led his Culpepper Minutemen across the bridge to the north bank of the river where they drove the British into their Fort Murray.[89]

There is a map that shows the sequence of events at the Battle at Great Bridge, Virginia, on 9 December 1775.[90]

---

87 Ibid.

88 Ibid.

89 Ibid., p. 15.

90 Battle of Great Bridge Map, Virginia, Southern Campaigns of the American Revolution, Vol. 4, No. 1, January - March 2007, Battle of Great Bridge by David K. Wilson, http://www.lib.jrshelby.com/scar.htm, p. 42, on 3/29/2008.

So ended a battle that had not lasted over a half hour. It was remarkable that no Patriot was killed and only one Patriot was wounded. Lieutenant Thomas Nash of the Norfolk County Militia suffered a slight wound to his hand. The casualties of the British were far greater. The Patriots buried Captain Fordyce with full military honors. Although the Battle of Great Bridge was brief, it was very significant. It cut off the British supply lines and Lord Dunmore and the British abandoned the south side of the mouth of Chesapeake Bay in the spring of 1776.[91]

On 10 December 1775, Colonel William Woodford in reference to the Battle of Great Bridge stated that :

". . . the victory was complete. . . . This was a second Bunker's Hill affair, in miniature, with this difference, that we kept our post and had only one man wounded in the hand."[92]

Another article on the Battle of Great Bridge includes the following:

"So why have most school children heard about the Battle of Bunker Hill but not the Battle of Great Bridge? The Historian Alf J. Mapp, Jr. of Portsmouth offers one reason.

The Battle of Great Bridge was quite significant. . . . Even George Washington recognized that. But you don't hear about it as much as you should."[93]

The Historian suggests that the views of American history were shaped in the early 19th century by textbook writers from New England. Thus, the battles fought in New England were given greater prominence than the battles elsewhere. An example of the New England mind-set is Noah Webster of dictionary fame who once stated that he decided standard pronunciations by using the pronunciations favored by cultivated people where he lived in New England.[94]

---

91 Wingo, Elizabeth B. and Hanbury, Elizabeth B., <u>The Battle of Great Bridge</u>, The Norfolk County Historical Society of Chesapeake, Virginia, and The Chesapeake Public Schools, March, 1998, p. 17.

92 Southern Campaigns of the American Revolution, Vol. 4, No. 1, January - March 2007, Battle of Great Bridge by David K. Wilson, http://www.lib.jrshelby.com/scar.htm, p. 49 on 3/29/2008. The cite for the magazine of the Southern Campaigns of the American Revolution is: http://www.southerncampaign.org.newsletter/v4n123.pdf.

93 The Battle of Great Bridge in a Furious and Bloody Half-Hour on Dec. 9, 1775, British Redcoats were Beaten by Colonials, http://scholar.lib.vt.edu, pp. 1 of 4, on 2/12/2008.

94 Ibid., p. 2.

It is interesting to note that the final draft of the Declaration of Independence was adopted by Congress just seven months later on July 4th, 1776.[95]

Another source stated that Colonel William Woodford, in charge of the 2nd Virginia Regiment, collected forces at Great Bridge of minutemen from Fauquier, Augusta and Culpepper counties in the western part of the Virginia Colony.[96]

Augusta County had been created out of Orange County in 1745, and Botetourt County had been created from Augusta County in 1770.[97]

"These elite militiamen from Virginia's western frontier were famed for their skill with the famous Kentucky long rifle."[98]

Kentucky Long Rifle History

A short history of the Kentucky long rifle follows:

"The great Kentucky flintlock-hunting rifle was more accurate than any known previous firearm and soon became famous. The history of Tennessee, Kentucky, and certainly the history of the United States, are each very much connected with the history of the Kentucky Long Rifle. This rifle is also known as the Kentucky, the hog rifle, or the long rifle. It was designed to be light, slender and graceful, and was the first truly American firearm. Created in the 1730s in Lancaster, Pennsylvania, by skillful immigrant craftsmen from Germany and Switzerland, the Kentucky rifle was the supreme implement created as a state of the art, ultimately for over a century, until the coming of the 'cap and ball' percussion rifle in 1840.

The guns of the first American colonists were not rifles at all. They were smoothbore flintlock muskets imported from Europe. For a number of reasons, these old muskets were

95 The World Book Encyclopedia (Field Enterprises Educational Corporation), Chicago, 1977, D Volume 5, p. 66.

96 Battle of Great Bridge - Wikipedia, the free encyclopedia, http://en.wikipedia.org/wiki/ Battle_of_Great-Bridge, p. 2 of 3, on 2/11/2008.

97 Researching Your Revolutionary War Ancestor, http://www.wvculture.org/HISTORY/ revwarbi.html, p. 1 of 8, on 3/29/2008.

98 Southern Campaigns of the American Revolution, Vol. 4, No. 1, January - March 2007, Battle of Great Bridge by David K. Wilson, http://www.lib.jrshelby.com/scar.htm, p. 43, on 3/29/2008.

not suitable for the American frontier. First of all, they were so heavy that to go hunting with one became a significant chore.

The Brown Bessies, as they were called, fired spherical balls of lead and required large balls in order to get weight and striking force. Their diameter was gauged from 0.60 to 0.70 inches in caliber, with corresponding robust recoil when fired. They were therefore wasteful of powder and lead, both being in short supply on the American frontier.

The large balls of the Bessies created other problems. They had high air-resistance, which slowed them greatly, giving them shorter range. Since the balls had no spin to balance the turbulence caused by slight surface imperfections, they curved viciously in flight, much like a pitched spitball does in the game of baseball. This unpredictable motion rendered these muskets ineffective beyond a range of 60 yards.

These assorted imperfections were prevailed over by the Lancaster gunsmiths. First they reduced the bores of the Kentucky to 0.45 to 0.50 caliber, so that one pound of lead, poured into iron molds, would produce from 70 to 120 round balls to be used for bullets, therefore, conserving valuable lead.

Next the barrel length was increased to 40 inches, in essence, so as to get extra thrust from the expanding gunpowder. The Kentucky Rifle had a greatly improved range compared to the Brown Bessie, which was fitted with a 30-inch barrel.

In its finality, the Kentucky was 'rifled,' with helical grooving in the barrel. This conveys rotary motion to the fired bullet on an alignment that coincided with the line of its flight trajectory. The spin gives rifles greater range and accuracy, compared to smoothbores.

The Kentucky Long Rifle was more accurate than any known previous firearm, and it soon became famous with a flight being deadly at over 200 yards, which was an astonishing range at the time.

The rifle became the primary weapon of the frontiersmen, especially in the isolated and hazardous wilds of Tennessee and Kentucky. The extensive use in Kentucky led to the adoption of the name 'Kentucky' for this rifle. Daniel Boone carried a Kentucky Rifle through Cumberland Gap.

During the Revolutionary War the British soldiers trained for volley shooting, and were fitted wholly with Brown Bessies; surprisingly, the volume of the American Armed Forces also carried muskets. **George Washington made a special effort to recruit frontiersmen who owned Kentucky Rifles.**

Advantages of the Brown Bessie muskets over the Kentucky Rifles were that they could be loaded easily and more rapidly than rifles, and did not require custom-made bullets. They would fire anything dropped down the barrel of the gun and would even function as a shotgun. Moreover, some of Washington's raw recruits were not good enough shots to require the extra accuracy of the Kentucky Rifle.

General Washington was able to assemble about 1,400 riflemen or backwoodsmen carrying Kentucky Rifles. *In training camps their feats of marksmanship astonished onlookers, some of whom were British spies. Word of these buckskin-wearing riflemen quickly spread to the British Army. Washington soon observed that the British gave his backwoodsmen wide latitude. As a hoax, he dressed up some of his musket-bearing soldiers in buckskins, knowing that the British assumed that anyone wearing frontier garb was carrying a Kentucky.*

Riflemen, when available, were used by the American Army as pickets and snipers. These skilled soldiers operated from the flanks of the regular Army. At the Battle of Saratoga in 1777, riflemen were used to pick off British officers. This feat greatly contributed to the American victory there, which was a decisive battle of the war.

The Battle of King's Mountain in 1780, another decisive victory, was won by rifle-toting backwoodsmen. These heroes were quickly gathered together from the neighboring southern Appalachians. At the close of the war, a British captain wrote in effect that the Americans had riflemen who could hit a man anywhere they liked at 200 paces. He suggested that at King's Mountain the mountain men whipped the British troops. . . .

The Kentucky Rifle was considered to be a necessity by frontiersmen, and practically every frontier family owned one. Rifle shooting was a way of life on the great American frontier, and nearly every settlement had a shooting match on weekends and holidays. The rifle was thus used for recreation, as well as for protection and hunting."[99]

Compiler's Conclusions Relative to Third Tour of Duty

I think it is fair to conclude that James Lambert was a young frontiersman with good eyesight and rifle expertise, being from Augusta County, Virginia. As a result of his rifle marksmanship skills, he was highly recruited by military officers under the leadership of General George Washington during the Revolutionary War. James Lambert undoubtedly was the owner of a Kentucky Long Rifle.

---

99 Bogan, Dallas, <u>A Short History of the Kentucky Long Rifle</u>, http://www.tngenweb.org, pp. 1-3 of 5, on 2/29/2008.

Thus, we have learned from James Lambert that his third tour of duty, like his second tour of duty, was within the Colony of Virginia. He commenced his third tour of duty in November of 1775 as a substitute for Jacob Ellsworth and his travels put him at the location and time of the Battle of Great Bridge on 9 December 1775. The officers James Lambert mentioned relative to this tour of duty included Colonels Crawford and Hillyard, Majors Hamilton and White, Captain Spencer, Ensign William Bryan and 1st Lt. or Sergeant Hilldepeny.[100]

It is my opinion that James Lambert was at that time an expert rifleman with one of the four companies of 50 soldiers each in the Augusta Militia Battalion of the District that consisted of Albemarle, Amherst, Augusta and Buckingham counties.

The Augusta Militia Battalion of 500 soldiers between the ages of 16 to 50 were supposed to muster four days each month, excepting December, January and February.

As a result of the decision in July 1775 to authorize two regiments of regular troops and sixteen battalions of minutemen for the better defense of Virginia against invasions and insurrection, the largest battalion formed was in the Culpeper Militia District, which was comprised of Culpeper, Orange and Fauquier counties. By September 1775, about 300 men had been recruited and divided into companies. The Commission of Safety commissioned Lawrence Taliaferro of Orange County to be Colonel, and Edward Stevens of Fauquier County to be Major of the battalion. They also commissioned ten captains for the companies into which the battalion was distributed.[101]

A write-up on the Battle of Great Bridge stated in part the following:

"Slowed by the lack of tents and provisions, on Saturday, December 2, Colonel Woodford with the 2nd Virginia Regiment and five companies of the Culpeper Minutemen (Buford, Jameson, Pickett, Chilton and Spencer) under Colonel Edward Stevens, who had marched from Hampton, arrived in the vicinity of the Great Bridge, which crossed the southern Branch of the Elizabeth River, some twelve miles southeast of Norfolk. . . . . . . one offensive move on the part of the Virginians was to be made. Lt. Col. Edward Stevens, of the Culpeper Minutemen, without a single loss, led a dash of 100 men, chiefly riflemen, to the battery entrenchments on the eastern peninsula. Leslie's position was now compromised

---

100   See Appendix, Item 3, pp. 124 and 126.

101   THE FORMATION OF THE MINUTE BATTALION, by Kyle Willyard, copyright 1995 http://www.liming.org/nwta/culform.html, p. 1 of 2, on 2/21/2008.

and the sharpshooters began picking tories and blacks off the bridge. The captain therefore withdrew his men and cannon into the fort, where his nephew, Lt. Peter Leslie, died in his arms. . . .Great Bridge was the first decisive battle fought in the South. Volunteer soldiers and militia had withstood a cannon supported attack by some of the finest professional soldiers in the world and virtually annihilated them. It is also one battle in the American Revolution where the riflemen played a very important role.[102]

". . .On October 24th, the Committee of Safety placed the 2nd Virginia Regiment, under the command of Colonel William Woodford, on alert. To the 2nd Virginia it attached five companies from the Culpeper Minute Battalion (Abraham Buford's, James Jamerson's William Pickett's, John Chilton's and Joseph Spencer's). The combined force was then ordered to the 'Neighbourhood of Norfolk or Portsmouth.'"[103]

James Lambert stated in his Amended Declaration (13 May 1844) that Captain Spencer was one of his officers in his second and third tours of military duty, commencing in July 1775 and ending in April or May 1776. He further stated that Captain Spencer discharged him in October 1775 at the end of his second tour of duty.[104]

Based upon the statements of James Lambert and my analysis, it seems reasonable to conclude that James Lambert was a member of the Augusta County Militia between July 1775 and April or May 1776. As a frontiersman from western Virginia, he was recruited with other rifle sharpshooters to join the forces of the 2nd Virginia Regiment in the area of Norfork and Great Bridge, Virginia, in November and December 1775, and there he was under the leadership of Colonel William Woodford, Lt. Colonel Edward Stevens and Captain Joseph Spencer.

At the Battle of Great Bridge, Virginia, on 9 December 1775, one can easily visualize that James Lambert was one of the 100 sharpshooters who charged the British under the command of Lt. Colonel Edward Stevens of the Culpeper Minutemen and forced the British to retreat from the bridge to their Fort Murray.

---

102   GREAT BRIDGE, by Kyle Willyard, http://www.liming.org/nwta/culbridge.html, pp. 1, 3, and 4 of 5, on 2/21/2008.

103   HAMPTON, by Kyle Willyard, http://www.liming.org/nwta/culhampton.html, p. 1 of 3, on 2/21/2008.

104   See Appendix, Item 3, p. 124.

Based upon the fact that Captain Spencer discharged James Lambert when his second tour of duty ended in October 1775, it seems logical to assume that James Lambert was in Captain Joseph Spencer's Company at the Battle of Great Bridge.[105]

It has been reported that Captain Joseph Spencer's place of birth was Orange County, Virginia, in 1744/45, and he died August 1829 in Grant County, Kentucky.[106] Captain Joseph Spencer is also considered to be a Patriot by the National Society of the Sons of the American Revolution.[107] Captain Joseph Spencer of the Virginia Line was a pensioner in Grant County, Kentucky, being granted a $240. pension effective 28 May 1818. He was age 84 at the time of his application and he died on 27 August 1829.[108]

You will recall an earlier mention that Lieutenant Robertson of Augusta County joined the service in 1775 and was in many battles, including the Battle of Great Bridge. Needless to say, there were many soldiers from Augusta County who participated at the Battle of Great Bridge, including James Lambert.

James Lambert also stated in his Amended Declaration (13 May 1844) that he was discharged at the end of his third military tour of duty by Colonel Crawford.[109]

Colonel William Crawford was:

"Born in Westmoreland County, Pennsylvania, in 1722. His father died in 1725, and his widow married Richard Stephenson. . . William married Hannah Vance in 1744. The Crawfords lived in Berkeley County on the Bullskin on land taken in 1747. . . .

Crawford served under Washington in the Indian wars. He was lieutenant-colonel of the Fifth Virginia, February 13, 1776; colonel of the Seventh Virginia, August 14, 1776. Fought at Trenton, Princeton, Brandywine, and Germantown. Resigned March 22, 1777. Later served on the western frontiers of Virginia, led an expedition against the Indians,

---

105   The Discharge of the Battalion, by Kyle Willyard, http://www.liming.org/nwta/ culdischarge.html, p. 2 of 3, on 2/20/2008.

106   Joseph Spencer - Ancestry.com, http://trees.ancestry.com, on 3/4/2008.

107   Family Group Record for Joseph Spencer, SAR Patriot Index Edition III Database, copyright 1995-2002, National Society of the Sons of the American Revolution.

108   TIPS#157 - REV. WAR - GRANT, GRAVES, GRAYSON, GREEN, GREENUP, & HANCOCK COS., ftp://ftp.rootsweb.com, p. 1 of 4, on 3/4/2008.

109   See Appendix, Item 3, p. 126.

was captured, tortured, and burned at the stake in Wyandotte County, Ohio, June 11, 1782."[110]

In December of 1775, the Virginia General Assembly voted to increase the size of its forces from two regiments to nine regiments. These new regiments were to contain ten companies of sixty men each, three companies to be riflemen. The Fifth Regiment of the Virginia troops was stationed at Richmond Courthouse during the period from March 1776 until July 1776.[111]

Another source documented that the 5th Virginia Regiment was authorized on December 28, 1775; assigned to the Southern Department on February 27, 1776; organized at Richmond Court House on February 28, 1776, to consist of 10 companies from Westmoreland, Spotsylvania, Northampton, Chesterfield, Henrico, Bedford and Loudoun counties; relieved on September 3, 1776 from the Southern Department. . . .[112]

Therefore, it is my conclusion that after the Battle of Great Bridge James Lambert was transferred as a rifleman to the newly formed 5th Virginia Regiment, and that he was discharged by the then Lieutenant Colonel William Crawford in the area of Richmond, Virginia, at the end of his third military tour of duty as a substitute for Jacob Ellsworth in May of 1776.

---

110   Johnston, Ross B., <u>West Virginians in the American Revolution</u>, http://www.ancestry.com, pp. 68 and 69, on 3/4/2008.

111   History - Fifth Virginia Regiment, http://www.fieldmusic.com/fifth/history.php, p. 1 of 2, on 3/5/2008.

112   The 5th Virginia Regiment in the Revolutionary War, http://www.myrevolutionarywar. com/states/va/va-05.htm,p. 1 of 2, on 3/5/2008.

Fourth Military Tour of Duty Volunteered for Two Years from 1779 to 1781 at Ages 21 to 23 Battles of Cowpens (17 Jan 1781) and Guilford Court House (15 Mar 1781)

According to his Amended Declaration (13 May 1844), James Lambert entered the service once again some three years after his last discharge in May of 1776. This time he joined in the Spring of 1779 as a volunteer for a period of two years. He first served in the Company of Captain Andrew Johnson for some time before he was transferred to the command of Captain Christman. James also mentioned that he served in a third Company; however, he could not recall the Captain's name.[113]

It has been reported that Captain Isaac Hinkle, a soldier of ability and an Augusta (now Pendleton) County neighbor of James Lambert, was named Captain in 1781 in place of his brother-in-law, Andrew Johnson, who was given another command.[114] Hannah, a daughter of Justus Hinkle and a sister of Isaac Hinkle, had married a man with the surname of Johnson.[115] As mentioned earlier, the List of Isaac Henkle for the 1784 Census of Rockingham County, Virginia, being Page 7, included an Andw Johnston (Andrew Johnson), as a Head of Family, making him a neighbor of Isaac Hinkle, James Lambert and others.[116] It was reported on 21 March 1779 that an Alexander Robertson was in Captain Johnston's (Johnson's) Company.[117] Thus, it is reasonable to assume that this was the Captain Andrew Johnson who headed up the Company James Lambert joined in the Spring of 1779.

---

113   See Appendix, Item 3, p. 124.

114   Johnston, Ross B., West Virginians in the American Revolution, http://www.ancestry.com, p. 133, on 3/4/2008.

115   Mortons Pendleton County Families [E-H], http://www.geocities.com/Heartland/6173/MortE_H.htm, p. 12 of 15, on 5/4/2007.

116   Census - Henkle, http://www.rootsweb.com~varockin/censusih.htm, p. 1 of 2, on 5/9/2007.

117   Chronicles of the Scotch-Irish Settlement in Virginia, Volume 1, Augusta County Court Records, Order Book No. XVI, pp.205-207, 21 March 1779, http://www.rootsweb.com/~chalkley/volume_1/or16_205.htm, p. 3 of 3, on 4/5/2008.

The List of Anthony Rader for the 1784 Census of Rockingham County, Virginia, being Page 8, included a Captain George Christman, as a Head of Family.[118] It is my assumption that James Lambert was transferred during his fourth tour of duty to a Company under the command of this Captain George Christman.

With respect to this 4th tour, James Lambert recalls that he was marched to Richmond, Virginia, and was quartered in the Capitol for three months. He was engaged frequently as a scout and he took shipping at Rockets Landing, two miles from Richmond, and went to Norfolk. He stayed there several weeks before he was transported by water in the fall of 1779 to West Point, New York, on the North River. He was quartered at West Point during the cold winter of 1779-1780 and he was engaged in building block houses.[119]

At this time, the Continental Army of the American Revolutionary War was organized into six regional departments for command and administrative purposes; namely, the Main Army (also known as the Middle Department), Eastern Department, Northern Department, Southern Department, Western Department and Highland's Department.

"SOUTHERN DEPARTMENT included Virginia, North Carolina, South Carolina, and Georgia along with the western frontier south of Virginia. This department was the most independent of the commands due to geography and the need for year around operations. Most of the northern departments suspended offensive operations for the winter and early Spring. It also was the only one whose command structure was destroyed twice. The first time at the surrender of Charlestown on May 12, 1780. The second was at the Battle of Camden (South Carolina) on August 16, 1780.

HIGHLAND'S DEPARTMENT was the smallest in area, and was formed around the defenses on the Hudson River north of New York (City). After the British occupied New York City the defenses just north of there became critically important. The presences of British naval forces at New York emphasized the importance of the Hudson River, and both sides in the war recognized the importance of controlling that waterway. The Americans created fortifications, including West Point with its chain across the River. The British sought to gain control with the Saratoga Campaign in 1777."[120]

---

118   Census - Rader, http://www.rootsweb.com/~varockin/censusar.htm, p. 3 of 4, on 5/9/2007.

119   See Appendix, Item 3, p. 126.

120   Military Departments in the American Army, http://www.myrevolutionarywar.com/units-american/department.htm, pp. 1, 2 and 3 of 4, on 4/3/2008.

"The enlistments of most soldiers in the Continental Army of 1775 expired on the last day of the year. On 1 January, 1776, a new army was established. General Washington had submitted recommendations for reorganization to the Continental Congress almost immediately after accepting the position of Commander-in-Chief (June 15, 1775), but these took time to consider and implement. Despite attempts to broaden the recruiting base beyond New England, the 1776 army remained skewed toward the Northeast both in terms of its composition and geographical focus. . .[121]

"Because of manpower shortages, the Continental Army often worked in conjunction with state-controlled militia units, which were called out for short periods as needed."[122]

In July 1776 the 1st and 3rd Virginia Regiments of the Southern Department were assigned to the Main Army and 4th, 5th and 6th Virginia Regiments of the Southern Department were also assigned to the Main Army in September 1776.[123]

"In December 1776, the 2nd Virginia Regiment was ordered to join Washington's Main Army in New Jersey. Colonel Woodford was promoted to brigadier general and Alexander Spotswood became colonel of the 2d Virginia Regiment on February 21, 1777. . . .

Colonel Spotswood resigned after the Battle of Germantown to return to Virginia to take care of the family as he mistakenly thought his brother had been killed (he had in fact been wounded and captured). He was replaced by Colonel Christian Febiger, a Danish-born officer, who would command the regiment the rest of its existence. The 2nd Virginia Regiment entered winter quarters at Valley Forge, emerging in June 1778 to fight at the Battle of Monmouth on June 28, 1778. The Philadelphia Campaign had left the Virginia Line in shambles, depleting both men and supplies. On September 14, 1778, the 2nd Virginia Regiment is officially consolidated with the 6th Virginia Regiment to make a 'new' 2d Virginia Regiment. Colonel Febiger retains his command and Lt. Colonel Simms of the 6th Virginia Regiment becomes his new second in command. Even with this new consolidation, the regiments were under strength, and from this point forward would never operate as a 'regiment' again. While encamped around New York City in both the Hudson Highlands and Northern New Jersey, officers deemed supernumerary were given new assignments (while officially holding their prior titles) and parties of men would be assigned duties under various captains. A return written by Inspector General Steuben

---

121   List of Continental Army units - Wikipedia, the free encyclopedia, http://en.wikipedia. org,, p. 4 of 12, on 4/4/2008.

122   Ibid., p. 1 of 12.

123   Ibid., pp. 6 and 7 of 12.

indicates that the regiment only had 180 rank and file, which could form two divisions. It was decided that it would brigade with the 5th and 11th Virginia Regiments to 'compose a Battalion' and that these three regiments would 'furnish 61 Men for the Light Infantry'. This light infantry 'company' would be attached to Wayne's Corps of Light Infantry and took part in the storming of Stony Point in July 1779. Colonel Febiger would be one of these 'supernumerary' officers and assigned to command one of the composite battalions of light infantry in this attack. . . .

At this point, regimental history becomes very confusing to track. Given the number of men fit for duty, these 'regiments' are not really 'regiments' at all any more, yet they are still named as such. . . ."[124]

In 1777 the Virginia Line was assigned a quota of 15 regiments, being Virginia Regiments 1 through 15; however, this number was reduced to 11 in 1779.[125]

Battle of Stony Point, New York, on 16 July 1779

"In late May, 1779, British Lieutenant General Sir Henry Clinton sent a force of about 8,000 men up the North (or Hudson) River with the intention of drawing General George Washington's Continental Army out of its lair at West Point. By June 1st Crown (British) forces had occupied and begun fortifying Stony Point, New York on the west side of the river and Verplanek's Point on the east side. This move effectively closed King's Ferry, a major river crossing at that narrow point in the river, about 10 miles (16km) south of West Point and 35 miles (56 km) north of New York City. . . .

Washington (George) . . . formulated a plan of attack and selected a commander to lead it – Major General Anthony Wayne of Pennsylvania. . . .

Washington's plan called for a two-pronged, pincer-type, nighttime attack on the fortifications to be carried out by 1,200 men of his Corps of Light Infantry. . . .

Wayne himself was struck in the head by a spent musket ball and fell to the ground, leaving Col. Christian Febiger to take over command of Wayne's column. . . .

The battle had lasted less than an hour, yet it proved to be the major engagement of 1779, and one of the last major battles of the War in the Northern theater."[126]

---

124   2nd Virginia Regiment - Wikipedia, the free encyclopedia, http://en.wikipedia.org/ wiki/2nd_Virginia_Regiment, pp. 2 and 3 of 4, on 4/4/2008.

125   List of Continental Army units - Wikipedia, the free encyclopedia, http://en.wikipedia. org, p. 10 of 12, on 4/4/2008.

126   Battle of Stony Point - Wikipedia, the free encyclopedia, http://en.wikipedia.org/wiki/ Battle_of_Stony_Point, pp. 1, 2 and 3 of 4, on 3/20/2008.

Not only was the 1st and 2nd Virginia Regiments involved in the Battle of Stony Point, but a company of soldiers from Augusta County, Virginia, also participated. General Wayne commanded a brigade of four regiments, one of which was from Virginia. The field officers of this regiment were Colonel Febiger, Lieutenant-Colonel Fleury, and Major Posey. One of the companies of the Virginia regiment was commanded by Captain Robert Gamble of Augusta County, Virginia.[127]

The 1st and 2nd Virginia Regiments were reorganized on 22 July 1779 in the Hudson Highlands.[128]

Although James Lambert did not arrive in the Hudson Highlands area until the fall of 1779 and after the Battle of Stony Point, there was already a presence in the area of Virginia Regiments which even included Captain Robert Gamble's Company from Augusta County, Virginia.

Background on West Point, New York

General George Washington considered the site of West Point to be so strategic and significant during the American Revolution that he called it the key to the continent. Washington felt that if the British ever commanded the fortifications at West Point they would have a stranglehold on the colonies. He spent a significant portion of his tenure as Commander of the Continental Army at West Point and nearby Newburgh.[129]

The command of the forces in and near the Hudson Highlands had assumed such proportions as to require a Major-General for its head; thus, Major-General Israel Putnam was directed to relieve General McDougall early in the month of May 1777.[130]

---

127   Waddell's Annals of Augusta County, Virginia, from 1726 to 1871, Chapter 10: The War of the Revolution, etc., from 1779 to 1781, p. 266, http://www.roanetnhistory.org, p. 1 of 2, on 3/19/2008.

128   Wright, Jr., Robert K., The Continental Army, Chapter 6, Professionalism: New Influences From Europe, p. 147, http://www.history.army.mil.books.RevWar/ContArmy/CA-06.htm, p. 21 of 23, on 4/3/2008.

129   West Point, NY – A Site on a Revolutionary War Road Trip on US Route 9W, http://www.revolutionaryday.com/usroute9w/westpoint.default.htm, pp. 5 and 6 of 8, on 4/5/2008.

130   Boynton, Edward C., History of West Point And Its Military Importance During The American Revolution: And The Origin And Progress Of The United States Military Academy, Kessinger Publishing, Whitefish, Montana, Chapter III, p. 43.

The project of strengthening the defenses in the Hudson Highlands lacked leadership when Major-General Israel Putnam filed a less than satisfactory progress report, dated 13 February 1778, to his Commander-in-chief and left West Point the next day for Connecticut to attend to some private affairs.[131]

In order to get the project back on track, General Washington ordered Major-General McDougall to assume the chief command again at Hudson Highlands and he arrived and assumed the command on the 28th of March 1778.[132]

Colonel Rufus Putnam, a cousin of Major-General Israel Putnam, arrived at West Point at the same time with his 5th Massachusetts Regiment. He had been appointed by Congress in 1778 as an Engineer with the rank of Colonel. He had resigned that appointment to take command of the 5th Massachusetts Regiment on 8 December 1776.[133]

Thaddeus Kosciuszko, having also been appointed by Congress in 1776 as an Engineer with the rank of Colonel, arrived at West Point on the 26th of March 1778.

Since Colonel Rufus Putnam and Colonel Thaddeus Kosciuszko had worked together under General Gates at the North, they were a very good combination to get the project back on track to enhance the fortifications at West Point.[134]

"In his The Hudson From the Wilderness to the Sea, Benson Lossing gives a clear account of this Revolutionary Fort (Fort Putnam) as it looked in 1866:

'Fort Putnam was erected by the Americans in 1778, for the purpose of defending Fort Clinton, on West Point below, and to thoroughly secure the river of hostile fleets. It was built under the direction of Colonel Rufus Putnam, and chiefly by the men of his Massachusetts regiment. It commanded the river above and below the Point, and was almost impregnable, owing to its position. . . . Redoubts were also built upon other eminences in the vicinity. . . .'"[135]

A profile on Colonel Rufus Putnam reads as follows:

131 Ibid., Chapter IV, pp. 59 and 60.
132 Ibid., p. 62.
133 Ibid., pp 62 and 63.
134 Ibid.
135 Fort Putnam, http://www.hhr.highlands.com/putnam.htm, p. 1 of 1, on 3/18/2008.

"*Colonel Rufus Putnam, Chief Engineer, Continental Army (April 1776-December 1776): Rufus Putnam was born April 9, 1738, in Sutton, Massachusetts. A millwright by trade, his three years of Army service during the French and Indian War influenced him to study surveying and the art of war. After the Battle of Lexington (19 April 1775), he was commissioned an officer of the line, but General Washington soon discovered his engineering abilities. He planned the fortifications on Dorchester Neck that convinced the British to abandon Boston. Washington then brought Putnam to New York as his Chief Engineer. He returned to the infantry service in 1777, taking command of the 5th Massachusetts Regiment. He and his troops helped to fortify West Point, erecting strong defenses atop the steep hill that commanded that garrison. The remains of Fort Putnam, preserved by the Military Academy, still honor his name there. Putnam was named a brigadier general in the Continental Army in 1783. In 1788 he led the first settlers to found the present town of Marietta, Ohio. The fortifications that he built there saved the settlements from annihilation during the disastrous Indian wars. He became Surveyor General of federal public lands and judge of the Supreme Court of Ohio. He died in Marietta on May 1, 1824.*"[136]

"*Kosciusko was at West Point for almost two and a half years and strengthening what Washington considered the 'key to America.' . . . .During most of the twenty-eight months he spent at West Point, Kosciusko devoted his time and energy to strengthening the fortifications and doing what he could to alleviate the shortages of food, clothing, and comforts for his men. Writing to one of Washington's aides during the bitter winter of 1779-80, he again complained of having insufficient manpower to do the job and had to plead as well for basic necessities for his workmen.*

I beg you to inform [his Excellency] I have but Eighty fatigue men for all the works of West Point and I expect less and less every day: this will be the Cause, that the works will not be Completed and not to be imputed to my neglect. . . . I have three masons from the Virginia line, and [they] are best mason of few number that I have. I should beg to keep them, but as they are in Great want of shoes, I will thank you to procure an order for three pairs of shoes on the Commissary of the Clothing at Newburgh."[137]

You will recall that, according to James Lambert, he was shipped by water from Norfolk, Virginia, to West Point, New York, in the fall of 1779. Therefore, he arrived

---

136   Portraits and Profiles Chief Engineer - 1775 to Present, http://www.hq.usace.army.mil/history/coe.htm, pp. 2 and 3 of 10, on 4/9/2008.

137   AmericanHeritage.com/Kosciusko, http://www.americanheritage.com, pp. 5 and 6 of 10, on 3/18/2008.

at West Point after the Battle of Stony Point, New York, on 16 July 1779 and before the cold winter of 1779-1780.

James specifically stated in his Amended Declaration (13 May 1844) that:

". . . . he went to West Point on the North river, quartered there the winter of 1780 (the cold winter) and was engaged in building Block Houses. He sailed from Norfolk for West Point in the fall of the year."[138]

"The winter of 1778-79 had been unusually mild and gave no hint as to what was to come. The winter of 1779-1780 would abound with problems for the Northern army. Not only would the winter be unusually severe (New York harbor froze over) but quarters were not available to protect the men from the cold. Nor was there adequate food, clothing or even blankets on hand, nor the hard cash to purchase these items locally. The result was poor morale, frost bite, sickness and death, and some mutinous actions.

Disposition of the Patriot Armies for the winter was made by Washington in the North and Lincoln in the South. The main army under Washington went to Morristown. A lesser force was assigned to Danbury, Connecticut, for the winter. They were to protect the area from sea borne ground forces as had previously occurred at New Haven and other coastal towns. A third force remained to protect West Point and the river passage while General Lincoln remained in Charleston with his army."[139]

A more graphic description of the cold winter of 1779-1780 reads as follows:

"The winter of 1780 was the worst in living memory. Soldiers of the West Point garrison were forced to eat their shoe leather; no camp dogs survived the long, lean winter. The Hudson froze solid all the way to the ocean, and a troop of cavalry rode across the ice from Staten Island to Manhattan."[140]

In the autumn of 1779, the garrison at West Point consisted of two Massachusetts brigades on the Point; the Connecticut line on the east side of the river; and the North Carolina brigade on Constitution Island. The light infantry and the Maryland line were encamped from Fort Montgomery northward, and Nixon's brigade occupied

---

138   See Appendix, Item 3, p. 126.
139   Revolutionary War - November 1779, http://revolutionarywararchives.org/ 49november1779.html, p. 2 of 4, on 3/18/2008.
140   Plebes Along the Hudson (cont.), http://historictraveler.away.com, p. 1 of 3, on 3/18/2008.

the Continental Village. In the assignment of the army to winter quarters, the Massachusetts line were left to garrison West Point and the Hudson Highlands, the command of which General Heath assumed on the 28th of November, 1779.[141]

"The winter of 1779 and 1780 was one of unexampled severity at West Point. The troops, except those on garrison duty, were cantonized in huts two miles back of West Point, on the 'public meadows,' and at 'Budd's,' on the east side of the river. So intense was the cold, that for a period of forty days, no water dripped from the roofs which sheltered them.

The snow was four feet deep on a level, requiring a heavy force to be constantly engaged in keeping open the communication with the six or seven redoubts built and building. Twice during the winter the North Redoubt barely escaped total destruction by fire. The parapet, built of logs, covered with earth, and difficult of access, burned nearly three days before the fire could be extinguished. . . .

On the 21st of February, General Heath obtained a leave of absence, and being shortly afterward appointed by the State of Massachusetts to superintend the recruiting service, the command at West Point was transferred, early in April, to General Robert Howe. Throughout the spring of 1780, the movements of the enemy so fully impressed the Commander-in-chief with their intention to assail West Point, that he directed Generals McDougall and Steuben to repair thither. The garrison was reinforced, and the army moved up to cover the entrance of the Highlands."[142]

It is little wonder that James Lambert, having personally experienced the severe winter of 1779-1780 at West Point, New York, could vividly remember some 64 years later these circumstances he experienced at the youthful ages of 21 and 22.

It is also apparent that James remembered helping to build block houses and redoubts during his stay at West Point.

According to the original plan Kosciuszko proposed in 1778, blockhouses were built inside the redoubts. A redoubt is a small fortification designed to protect an important feature such as a hill or pass and it contains infantry and often cannon. With respect to Redoubt 4 which was located on a hill west of Fort Putnam, Kosciuszko submitted

---

141   Boynton, Edward C, see prior footnote 130, Chapter V, p. 85.
142   Ibid., pp. 85 and 86.

plans as early as 6 February 1779. General McDougall provided the following specific instructions on 25 April 1779:

- Make blockhouse bombproof

- Size not to exceed quarters for 100 men

- If practicable, build the cellar to hold 30 days of supplies (previous standard was 14 days)

- Enclose the blockhouse in a redoubt

- Parapet should withstand artillery, especially from the west[143]

An attempt was made to erect the blockhouse in Redoubt 4 in the spring of 1780 but the ground was still too hard to dig. Redoubt 4 was apparently inspected by Major-General Benedict Arnold on 25 September 1780 and his notes indicated that there were two cannon (six pounders); a garrison for 100 men (probably safe from surprise attack due to good observation); wood wall 10 inches high and 4-5 inches thick and west wall faced with stone; but not bombproofed.[144]

On the 3rd of August, 1780, Major-General Benedict Arnold had been instructed from general head-quarters at Peekskill, to proceed to West Point and relieve General Robert Howe of the command of that Post, and its dependencies.[145]

It is my belief from this research and collected information that James Lambert was engaged in the building of blockhouses at West Point in 1779 and 1780 and that he more than likely was involved in the construction of the blockhouse in Redoubt 4.

Statement of Lemuel Hungerford (23 July 1841)

Lemuel Hungerford of Ross Township, Butler County, Ohio, appeared before John Ashby, a Justice of the Peace, in Hamilton County, Ohio, on 23 July 1841, and stated under oath that he served in the militia with James Lambert in the years 1779 and 1780 under Captain Spencer at West Point, Captain Cary at Horse Neck and Captain Adam Shapley at New London.[146]

---

143   Redoubt 4–West Point, http://www.unc.edu/~chaos1/redoubt4.html, p. 1 of 3, on 3/18/2008.

144   Ibid., p. 2 of 3.

145   Boynton, Edward C, see prior footnote 130, Chapter VI, p. 87.

146   See Appendix, Item 1, p. 120.

You will recall that there was a Captain Joseph Spencer of the Virginia Line who was born in Orange County, Virginia, and participated in the Battle of Great Bridge. In fact, it is my speculation that this was the Captain Spencer who discharged James Lambert at the end of his second tour and that James Lambert was in Captain Spencer's Company at the Battle of Great Bridge. Although we now know that the 1st and 2nd Virginia Regiments were involved in the Battle of Stony Point, I have been unable to confirm that this Captain Joseph Spencer participated in that battle.

We now know from further research that Connecticut and Massachusetts lines were in the Hudson Highlands area in 1779 and 1780. We also know that a smaller part of Washington's main army was assigned to Danbury, Connecticut, for part of the winter of 1779-1780 to protect the coastal towns.

The 2nd Connecticut Regiment of the Continental Line was raised after the Battle of Lexington and Concord by Colonel Joseph Spencer, who was born in East Haddam, Middlesex County, Connecticut, in 1714. This Regiment was engaged in defending the Hudson Highlands in 1779 and a light infantry company from this Regiment was at the Battle of Stony Point on 16 July 1779. The Regiment's encampment during December 1779 to May 1780 was at Morristown, New Jersey.[147]

The 6th Connecticut Regiment was encamped on the Hudson Highlands across from West Point in the early part of 1779. This force successfully stormed the British Fort of Stony Point on the Hudson River on 15 July 1779. From Stony Point, the 6th Connecticut Regiment was stationed with the Connecticut Line around West Point where it worked again on fortifications in the area. The Morristown huts in New Jersey were the site of winter quarters for the two Connecticut Brigades in the winter of 1779-1780. The Connecticut Line spent the summer of 1780 along the Hudson River and while in Orangetown, New Jersey, heard of the treason of Connecticut's own General Benedict Arnold and his flight on September 25th. The Connecticut 6th Regiment was ordered to West Point to defend any attack the enemy might have planned. There was no attack and the Connecticut Line went into winter quarters near West Point.[148]

---

147   2nd Connecticut Regiment Home Page, http://www.revwar.com/2ndct/02ct.html, pp. 1 and 2 of 4, on 4/9/2008.

148   The 6th Connecticut Regiment - Battle History, http://www.6thconnecticut.org/ BATTLE.htm, pp. 2 of 2, on 5/10/2008.

In addition to Colonel Joseph Spencer of the 2nd Connecticut Regiment, both an Ebenezer Spencer and an Israel Spencer were born in Connecticut and were Captains in the Connecticut Line.[149]

In my opinion, Lemuel Hungerford's reference to a Captain Spencer at West Point was a reference to one of the three above mentioned officers in the Connecticut Line.

The Statement of Lemuel Hungerford (23 July 1841) also made reference to

"Captain Cary at Horse neck".... where I saw Mr. James Lambert ...."[150]

Major-General William Tryon (former Royal Governor of New York and North Carolina) led at least 600 British infantry troops from Kings Bridge, New York, on a raid of Horseneck Landing, Connecticut, on 26 February 1779. They brushed aside a small militia patrol at New Rochelle and went on to Horseneck, quickly overwhelming the 150-man militia guard there. After plundering the town they returned home with 200 head of cattle.[151]

You will recall that General Washington removed Major-General Israel Putnam as the chief commander at Hudson Highlands and General McDougall assumed command on 28 March 1778. Major-General Israel Putnam went to Connecticut to hasten the work of recruiting the army for the next campaign. During the years 1778-1779, he was engaged in the western part of Connecticut, with headquarters usually at Danbury, co-operating with the force in the Hudson Highlands. At this time he made his famous escape from General Tryon's troops by riding down the stone steps at Horse neck in the township of Greenwich.[152]

"On May 11, 1665, the General Assembly in Hartford declared Greenwich a separate township, and authorized funds for the hiring and support of an orthodox minister. In 1672, the so-called '27 Proprietors' bought land from the few remaining Indians to the west of the Myanos River.' This land became known as 'Horseneck' because of the neck of land now known as Field Point was the common HORSE PASTURE. Official title was

---

149   Family Group Records for Ebenezer Spencer, Israel Spencer and Joseph Spencer reproduced from SAR Patriot Index Edition III Database, Copyright 1995-2002, National Society of the Sons of the American Revolution.

150   See Appendix, Item 1, p. 120.

151   Battles 1779, http://www.rsar.org/military/bat-79.htm, p. 2 of 5, on 4/10/2008.

152   Israel Putnam, http://www.famousamericans.net/israelputnam, p.7 of 11, on 4/10/2008.

not obtained from the Indians until 1686, but the land was laid out for home lots, divided and granted to those so-called '27 Proprietors.

The town of Greenwich expanded and prospered steadily, supplying the packet boats with shipments of locally grown produce and other wares. Greenwich played an active role in the Revolutionary War. Its most famous event was the race through Greenwich by General Israel PUTNAM, who made a daring escape from the British on the morning of February 26, 1779. While the British were able to pillage and loot Greenwich, they were not able to prevent General PUTNAM from rushing to warn Stamford. General PUTNAM's tricorn hat, with a bullet hole pierced through its side, is displayed at 'Putnam's Cottage,' the tavern belonging to Israel KNAPP. General PUTNAM stayed in the tavern the night before his famous ride, and the site is now maintained as a museum by the DAR, and is located at 243 East Putnam Avenue, Greenwich, CT."[153]

Since the 6th Connecticut Regiment was encamped on the Hudson Highlands across from West Point in the early part of 1779, it was customary to send the 6th Connecticut Regiment to help defend its own state against British raids led by Major-General Tryon in 1779.[154]

According to James Lambert, he was marched from West Point to Horse neck on the East River where he remained for three months.[155]

The East River connects Upper New York Bay on its south end to Long Island Sound on its north end. It separates Long Island (including the boroughs of Queens and Brooklyn) from the island of Manhattan and the Bronx on the North American mainland.[156] Therefore, the East River flows into Long Island Sound which forms the southern boundary of Horseneck/Greenwich, Connecticut.

Although I have been unable to specifically identify a Captain Cary, it is quite possible that there was a Captain Cary either in the 6th Connecticut Regiment at West Point that was called to defend Horseneck/Greenwich, Connecticut, in 1779, or in another

---

153   Greenwich Connecticut History, http://www.rootsweb.ancestry.com, p. 1 of 2, on 4/12/2008.

154   The 6th Connecticut Regiment - Battle History, http://www.6thconnecticut.org/battle. htm, p. 2 of 3, on 4/3/2008.

155   See Appendix, Item 3, p. 126.

156   East River - Wikipedia, the free encyclopedia, http://en.wikipedia.org/wiki/East_River, p. 1 of 3, on 4/12/2008.

Connecticut military unit assigned to protect Horseneck/Greenwich, Connecticut, during the period of three months James Lambert was there in 1780.

The Statement of Lemuel Hungerford (23 July 1841) further made reference to

"*. . . . Captain Adam Shapley at Newlondon where I saw Mr. James Lambert.*"[157]

The <u>History of New London County, Connecticut</u>, indicates that the military organization for the coast defense was arranged anew for the year 1777. The three posts of New London, Groton, and Stonington were placed under the command of Major Jonathan Wells, of Hartford. Two companies were raised and stationed in New London, one of artillery, consisting of fifty men, of which Nathaniel Saltonstall was captain; the other of musketry, consisting of seventy men, of which Adam Shapley was Captain. In March 1778, Captain William Ledyard was appointed to the command posts of New London, Groton, and Stonington, with the rank and pay of major. Under his direction the works were repaired and strengthened and additional batteries erected. William Latham was captain of artillery at Groton, and Adam Shapley at New London. These appointments were not made by Congress or the commander-in-chief, but emanated from the Governor and Council of Safety. It is interesting to note that in February 1778 a detachment of Continental troops, under the command of Colonel Dearborn, was sent to aid the militia in the defense of New London.[158]

"Fort Trumbull occupies a key site in the approaches to New London Harbor. From its position it could fire upon any ship entering the Thames River and work in coordination with Fort Griswold on the Groton side of the river. Work was started on the present site of Fort Trumbull prior to the outbreak of the Revolution in 1775. On October 2nd, 1775 the Connecticut General Assembly ordered that the fort be completed in response to the outbreak of the Revolution. The superintendent of construction was Colonel Erastus Wolcott.

On April 10th, 1776 Commodore Esek Hopkins of the fledgeling United States Navy was asked to emplace cannon at Fort Trumbull. These guns were captured by the U.S. Marines at Nassau in the Bahama Islands earlier in the war.

---

157   See Appendix, Item 1, p. 120.

158   Hurd, D. Hamilton, The <u>History of New London County, Connecticut</u>, J. W. Lewis & Co., Philadelphia, 1882, Chapter 12 - New London Revolutionary War, pp. 168-181, http://www.dunhamwilcox.net/town_hist/nl-chap12.htm, pp. 17 and 18 of 22, on 4/10/2008.

On July 18th, 1777 Governor Trumbull ordered completion of the fort at New London (which the colony's assembly named after the governor). On March 25th, 1778 Major William Ledyard was placed in command of both Fort Trumbull and Fort Griswold.

The only combat in Fort Trumbull's history happened on September 6th, 1781. This was a diversionary raid to distract American and French forces from Yorktown where the British army surrendered the next month.

Fort Trumbull was garrisoned by only 23 men under the command of Captain Adam Shapley when it was attacked by British forces under the command of the infamous Benedict Arnold. In obedience to Colonel Ledyard's orders 'Shapley fired one well-aimed volley, spiked the six guns, and withdrew his men in good order to several whale boats that were tied at the shore. Shapley's men rowed furiously, but by now two British ships were so far up the harbor that the men on their decks could reach the whale boats with musket shot. In fact seven of the men were wounded and one of the boats captured.' (From the Connecticut Series in the New London Historical Society Collection.)

Shapley was later severly (severely) wounded defending Fort Griswold and died on February 14th, 1782 at the age of 43.

After seizing Fort Trumbull, the British attacked Fort Griswold on Groton Heights. After a valiant defense, most of the defenders of Fort Griswold were massacered by the British."[159]

The Ye Antientest Burial Place (Cemetery) in New London, Connecticut, contains a gravestone that reads as follows:

"Capt. Adam Shapley - Militia (Commander of Fort Trumbull Garrison, New London), Mortally wounded at Fort Griswold, died 5 months later, Age 43.

In Memory of Capt. Adam Shapley of Fort Trumbull who bravely gave his Life for his Country a fatal Wound at Fort Griswold Sept. 6th 1781 caused his Death Febry 14 1782 Aged 43 years. Shapley thy deed reverse the Common doom and make thy name imortal in a tomb"[160]

It has been reported that Lemuel R. Hungerford was born on 14 May 1759 in East Haddam, Middlesex County, Connecticut, and that he died on 21 Feb 1846 in Venice,

---

159   Fort Trumbull - A History, http://www.geocities.com/~jmgould/trumhist.html, pp. 1, 2, and 3 of 12, on 4/10/2008.
160   Known defender's final resting spots, http://www.revwar.com/ftgriswold/graves2.html, pp. 32 and 33 of 33, on 4/10/2008.

Butler County, Ohio. He married Abigail Beebe on 9 Nov 1785 in the town of his birth, and they had two sons; namely, John, born 31 Dec 1787, and Richard, born 8 Dec 1788.[161]

Lemuel Hungerford is included in a Tax List for the year 1807 in Butler County, Ohio.[162] He also is included in the 1820 United States Federal Census for Ross Township, Butler County, State of Ohio, apparently known to be living with his son, Richard, at that time.[163]

Lemuel Hungerford with the rank of private received a semi-annual pension allowance of $32.08 and payments were made to him in September 1831 and each March and September thereafter in the years 1832 through 1845.[164]

According to the Statement of Lemuel Hungerford (23 July 1841), he served with James Lambert in the militia in 1779 and 1780 under Captain Spencer at West Point, New York; Captain Cary at Horseneck, Connecticut; and Captain Adam Shapley at New London, Connecticut. As a result of my research, I believe these named officers were at these locations in 1779 and 1780 and that Lemuel Hungerford and James Lambert could well have served together under their leadership.

James Lambert stated that he left Horseneck/Greenwich, Connecticut, after a stay of three months and marched to Peekskill, New York, and then he marched back to Virginia, getting there at the time the cherries were ripe.[165]

Assuming one can pick ripe cherries in Virginia during the month of June, it would appear that James Lambert, starting his march from Peekskill, New York, in the spring of 1780, arrived back in Virginia in June, 1780.

The Southern Campaign

"In May of 1780, news of the fall of Charles Town, South Carolina, and the capture of General Benjamin Lincoln's southern army reached Congress. They voted to place (General

---

161   Lemuel R. Hungerford - Ancestry.com, http://trees.ancestry.com, p. 1 of 1, on 4/11/2008.
162   Ohio Census, 1790-1890 - Ancestry.com, http://search.ancestry.com, p. 1 of 2, on 4/11/2008.
163   1820 United States Census - Ancestry.com, http://search.ancestry.com, p. 1 of 2, on 4/11/2008.
164   Ancestry.com - U.S. Pensioners, 1818-1872, http://search.ancestry.com, Pension Office State - Ohio - Year Range 1831-1848, pp. 1 and 2 of 3, on 4/11/2008
165   See Appendix, Item 3, p. 126.

Horatio) Gates in command of the Southern Department. He learned of his new command at his home near modern Shepherdstown, West Virginia, and headed south to assume command of remaining Continental forces near Deep River in North Carolina on July 23, 1780.

He led continental forces and militia south, to their stand-up fight with British general Charles Cornwallis at the Battle of Camden on August 16, where he was overwhelmingly defeated. Gates' only notable accomplishment in the unsuccessful campaign was to cover 170 miles in three days on horseback, headed north in retreat. His bitter disappointment was compounded by the news of his son Robert's death in combat in October. Nathanael Greene replaced Gates as commander on December 3, and he (Gates) returned home to Virginia. Because of the debacle at Camden, Congress passed a resolution requiring a board of inquiry (prelude to a court martial) to look into Gates' conduct in that affair."[166]

Rugeley's Mill and Camden, South Carolina (August 1780)

James Lambert stated under oath that he was marched over the Haw River in order to get to North Carolina. He said the object was to secure General Gates who was then in the south. He then marched across the Dan, Deep and Pee Dee rivers and was quartered at Rugeley's Mill. Rugeley was said to be a tory. There he helped to take out flour for the American Army. James Lambert was also about ten miles from Camden, South Carolina, when that battle was fought on 16 August 1780. Although he was not in the Camden engagement, he was close enough to hear it.[167]

"On July 25 he (Gates) assumed command of his 'grand army'—1,520 Continentals and 8 cannons, at Hillsborough, N.C. Overruling the advice given him by his general officers, Gates began the advance on July 27 by the most direct route to Camden, S.C., even though the way ran through infertile, thinly-peopled, and an unfriendly portion of the country. On August 15 his army totaled about 4,100 men and six cannon—900 Continental and about 3,200 militia, but Gates for some reason thought he had 7,000 men. That night both Gates and Cornwallis, the British commander, decided to make — night attacks. About 2 a.m. on August 16, 1780 the two armies collided about 9 miles north of Camden. After an exchange of fire both forces formed lines of battle and waited for daylight to begin the action. Gates placed his Continentals on the right and his militia on the left. Cornwallis opened the action with a vigorious attack on the American left and at the first fire the militia

---

166   Horatio Gates - Wikipedia, the free encyclopedia, http://en.wikipedia.org/wiki/
         Horatio_Gates, pp. 2 and 3 of 4, on 4/12/2008.
167   See Appendix, Item 3, pp. 125 and 126.

threw away their arms and fled. Stationed 600 yards behind the line of battle, Gates was 'swept away' by this 'Torrent' of fleeing men and when he regained control of his horse that evening he found himself at Charlotte, N.C., 60 miles from the battlefield. Only 700 men from his army of 4,100 rejoined Gates at Hillborough and 650 of his Continentals were killed or captured in the battle.

Camden was one of the most crushing American defeats of the entire war and it ended all hope of establishing American power in Georgia and the Carolinas and also opened Virginia to invasion. On October 5, 1780 Congress voted that an inquiry be made into Gates' conduct and ordered Washington to appoint another commander of the Southern Department until that inquiry was held. General Nathanael Greene, selected by Washington, relieved Gates at Charlotte on December 2, 1780. Greene treated Gates with the utmost kindness and refused to hold the court of inquiry because his few general officers could not be spared for this purpose. Gates therefore withdrew to 'Traveller's Rest' where he remained during 1781, writing constantly to Washington and to Congress requesting that inquiry into his conduct be held. On August 5, 1782 Congress generously responded by repealing its resolve of October 5, 1780, and by ordering Gates to take such command in the main army as Washington should direct. Gates, his self-respect restored, set out for headquarters and during the remainder of the war was with Washington at the New Windsor Cantonment near Newburgh, N.Y. Retiring from the Continental Army on November 3, 1783, Gates returned to his Virginia home.

His only son died in 1780 and his wife in 1784. Gates married Mary Vallance, a Maryland heiress with a fortune of nearly $500,000, in 1786. In 1790 Gates emancipated his slaves, sold his Virginia plantation and moved to New York. There he took residence at 'Rose Hill Farm,' an area that is now bounded by 23rd and 30th Streets and 2nd and 4th Avenues in New York City. A Jeffersonian Republican during his last years, Gates served one term in the New York legislature, 1800-1801. He died at 'Rose Hill' on April 10, 1806."[168]

"Camden was central to controlling the back county of South Carolina because of its crossroads location near the Wateree River and the Catawba (Indian) Trail.

. . . . On August 9, General Cornwallis received word from Lord Rawdon of General Gates' approach and he immediately set out for Camden, arriving on August 13. Meanwhile, Gates had found the going difficult and anticipated supplies had not turned up along the

---

168   National Register of Historic Places Inventory - Nomination Form 10-300 (July 1969), General Horatio Gates House, "Traveler's Rest", http://www.wvculture.org/shpo/nr/pdf/ jefferson/72001288.pdf , pp. 7 and 8 of 13, on 4/14/2008.

route. The men ended up eating green apples and peaches. On August 15, General Gates issued orders for a night approach to Camden. The evening's meal had been topped off with a dessert of molasses that had dire effects on the digestion of the men. At the same time, General Cornwallis had ordered a night march in preparation for an early morning attack on Gates at Rugeley's Mill. As Gates' Continental force marched south on the evening of the 15th, men often broke ranks as the molasses took its gut-wrenching effect.

At about 2:00 A.M. on August 16, 1780, the Southern Continental Army under Maj. General Horatio Gates and the British Army under Lt. General Charles Cornwallis literally ran into each other on the Waxhaws road. The cavalry screens of Continental Colonel Charles Armand and Lt. Colonel Banastre Tarleton clashed and skirmished in the dark. The cavalry was pushed back into the marching columns causing confusion until 100 Virginia state troops maintained formation and steadied the Continentals.

Both sides, having been surprised by the encounter, withdrew to plan and wait for dawn. Following the early morning skirmish, the element of surprise was gone. It was learned from prisoners taken that the British force was 3,000 strong and commanded by General Cornwallis himself. General Gates immediately called a council of war with his officers to discuss what action to take. Although Maj. General Baron de Kalb had privately advised retreat, he said nothing at the council of war.

After a few moments of silence, militia Brig. General Edward Stevens declared that it was too late to do anything but fight. General Gates wanted to prove his worth as a skilled commander, so when no other advice was offered, he insisted on facing the British on open ground. Although both Gates and the British estimated the American forces to be nearly 7,000 men, the actual number was only about 3,000, nearly 2,000 of whom were inexperienced militia.

Before dawn broke, General Gates formed his men. The core of his force, 900 Maryland and Delaware regulars under General de Kalb, were arrayed to the right of the Waxhaws road. To the left (of) the road, were placed 1,800 North Carolina militia. On their left were 700 Virginia militia. Colonel Armand's cavalry was held in reserve behind the Virginians. Gates himself was stationed with the reserves sone 200 yards behind the battle line.

When the British appeared on the field, Lord Rawdon commanded his own Volunteers of Ireland, as well as Lt. Colonel Tarleton's British Legion cavalry on the British left wing opposite of General de Kalb. Following European military custom, both General Gates and General Cornwallis had placed their most experienced troops on the right wing. As a result, Lt. Colonel James Webster commanded the most seasoned British regiments on the right wing opposite Gates' militia. In hindsight it looks to be a recipe for disaster for Gates.

The British opened the battle by attacking with their right wing on the American left wing at the heart of the militia. Brig. General Edward Stevens ordered his men to fix bayonets, which as militia they had never done before. In the face of an aggressive bayonet charge from the British, first the Virginians and then the North Carolina militia fled before the British regulars could even reach them. Many dropped their muskets without having fired a shot.

While the rout was taking place on the American left wing, the right wing under Maj. General Baron de Kalb was attacking after receiving the order from Maj. General Horatio Gates. They had no idea how bad things were on the left wing, because the dawn's dead calm had left the smoke from gunfire lingering in a haze on the field. The Maryland and Delaware Continental regulars twice repulsed Lord Rawdon's Volunteers of Ireland and then launched a counterattack.

The Continental counterattack was successful with prisoners taken and the Volunteers' line nearly broken. Lt. General Cornwallis saw the action, rode up and rallied his men. Meanwhile, Lt. Colonel James Webster controlled his men on the British right wing. Instead of pursuing the fleeing militia, he wheeled to the left and continued his charge as a flanking movement against General de Kalb.

Only one militia unit held its ground. It was a North Carolina regiment that had been stationed the closest to the Delaware Continental regulars. Their steadfastest (steadfastness) was rewarded by being the first to be hit by Lt. Colonel Webster's flank attack. The militia unit fought well and was joined by Maryland regulars that had been called up from the reserve by General de Kalb. The Maryland regulars fought off Webster's attack, but now only about 800 Continentals were facing at least 2,000 British regulars.

The small force continued to fight bravely. The final blow came when General Cornwallis ordered Lt. Colonel Banastre Tarleton and his British Legion to attack the American rear. Under the cavalry charge the ranks finally broke. Some Continentals managed to escape through a nearby swamp. General de Kalb himself had taken eleven wounds before falling. The field was taken after an hour. Tarleton pursued the fleeing Americans for over twenty miles before finally turning back.

What of Maj. General Horatio Gates himself? After the militia broke and fled, Gates soon followed. Some reported that he did attempt to rally the retreating militia, but to no avail. What can be said is that Gates was in Charlotte, North Carolina, sixty miles away by the evening of August 16 only hours after the battle. He was in Hillsborough, North Carolina, 180 miles away, by August 19.

General Gates' actions were almost immediately questioned. After Maj. General Nathanael Greene replaced him in December, he returned home to Virginia to await a inquiry into his conduct at Camden. He would not hold another command for the rest of the war. He did return to active duty before the end to official hostilities, serving in General Washington's command staff, as he had at the start of the war.

It was estimated that of the 3,000 men that made up the American force, 2,000 fled without firing a shot. Somewhere around 800 men were captured or killed and the army's munitions were also taken, while the British only sustained about 350 casualties. This loss left Patriot morale in the South at a low and the region firmly under British control until General Greene built the Continental forces back up in early 1781. Even with the care of Lt. General Charles Cornwallis' personal physician, Maj. General Baron de Kalb died at Camden three days after the battle."[169]

A map shows the camp of the Southern Army commanded by Maj. Gen. Horatio Gates at Rugeley's on August 13-15, 1780.[170]

Another map illustrates the Camden battlefield on 16 August 1780.[171]

These maps indicated that Rugeley's was about 13 miles north of Camden and the battlefield was only about four and one-half miles south of Rugeley's. There is no question that, assuming James Lambert was at Rugeley's on 16 August 1780, he was well within hearing range of the sounds of the Battle of Camden.

Having transcribed the Amended Declaration of James Lambert (13 May 1844) and having studied the above quoted material, it is my informed opinion that James Lambert accompanied in late July 1780 the continental forces and militia General Gates led from Hillsborough, North Carolina, to Rugeley's Mill, South Carolina. The total force of 4,100 consisted of 900 continentals and 3,200 militia. It is reasonable to assume that James Lambert was one of the militia from Virginia. The Gates forces were camped at Rugeley's no later than August 13, 1780. It would appear that all 900 regulars and as many as 2,500 militia were actually involved directly in the Battle of Camden on August 16, 1780. At least 2,000 of the militia in the engagement were

169   The American Revolution (Camden), http://www./theamericanrevolution.org/battles/
       bat_camd.asp, pp. 2, 3, and 4 of 5, on 4/14/2008.
170   Map of Southern Army Camp at Rugeley's, South Carolina, http://battleofcamden.org/
       awc-cam-a,jpg, p. 1 of 1, on 4/14/2008.
171   Map of the Battle of Camden, South Carolina, http://battleofcamden.org/landers.gif, p.
       1 of 1, on 4/14/2008

inexperienced. If the total force was 4,100, then some 700 militia men were in the area but not directly involved in the Camden battle, and James Lambert, fortunately, was one of members of that group. According to the maps and assuming James Lambert was at Rugeley's at the time of the Camden battle, he was only four to five miles from the battle and well within hearing distance of the sounds of that battle.

After the Battle of Camden, James Lambert was marched to North Carolina and he joined the army of the southern commander General Gates at Hillsborough, North Carolina. According to the above quoted material, James Lambert was one of the 700 out of a force of 4,100 that rejoined General Gates at Hillsborough, North Carolina. There he remained for several weeks when he went to Charlotte and well remembered when General Greene addressed the command of the South which was in the fore part of the winter before the Battles of Cowpens and Guilford Court House.[172]

As quoted earlier, General Nathanael Greene became the Southern Commander and replaced General Gates, at Charlotte, North Carolina, on 2 December 1780. James Lambert could not have been more accurate with respect to this change in leadership, giving great credence that he was there at the time and that he personally witnessed this event.

Battle of Cowpens, South Carolina, on 17 January 1781

"Greene split his force in the face of a superior enemy by sending a flying army under the command of Brigadier General Daniel Morgan to threaten Cornwallis and bolster local militia support . . . .

The result was the Battle of Cowpens on 17 January 1781. Morgan soundly defeated Tarleton in the greatest patriot victory of the war in the South . . . ."[173]

The Continental Congress approved on 9 March 1781 that Brigadier General Daniel Morgan be the 5th recipient of the Congressional Gold Medal, the highest civilian honor bestowed by the United States legislature.[174]

"The Congressional Gold Medal is created by the United States Mint to specifically commemorate the person and achievement for which the medal is awarded. Each medal

---

172   See Appendix, Item 3, p. 126.

173   Biography of Nathanael Greene, http://members.aol.com/JonMaltbie/Biography.html, p. 3 of 4, on 4/28/2007.

174   List of Congressional Gold Medal recipients - Wikipedia, the free encyclopedia, http://en.wikipedia.org, p. 1 of 9, on 4/30/2007.

is therefore different in appearance and there is no standard design for the Congressional Gold Medal . . . .[175]

"On March 25, 1790 he (Brigadier General Daniel Morgan) finally received a gold medal which Congress had struck to honor him for his victory at Cowpens."[176]

James Lambert could not pretend to give in detail all that happened during this part of his service. He was frequently engaged in foraging parties and in scout work, being in many places the names of which he could not remember.[177]

James Lambert was marched to Cowpens, South Carolina, in early January 1781, and he:

". . . . was there in that Battle."[178]

He thought he saw Colonel Hillyard riding along the line with one arm hanging down shattered by a musket ball. He also mentioned one circumstance somewhat suspicious.

"A war medic was engaged in doing something to a man that had fallen by the shot of the enemy. He was in the attitude of stooping and a ball from a Swivel struck him on a straight line and literally split him open. One of my messmates, Thomas Warmsley, had the straps of his knapsack shot off and I had a ball strike my leg, but not to cause me to be laid-up. It was a flesh wound only, but I carry the scar to this day."[179]

"The swivel gun was a small cannon named for it's mechanism of attachment. It was about the only 18th century gun that was not a 'crew-served' weapon, although it's effectiveness was multiplied when manned by more than the gunner. Once mounted, almost always on a fixed base . . . . it may be pointed quickly to any quarter. But the swivel mechanism cannot stand heavy recoil, so the size, and hence effectiveness, of a swivel gun is severely limited."[180]

---

175   Congressional Gold Medal - Wikipedia, the free encyclopedia, http://en.wikipedia.org, p. 1 of 2, on 4/30/2007.

176   Cowpens National Battlefield - Daniel Morgan (U.S. National Park Service), http://www.nps.gov/cowp/historyculture/daniel-morgan.htm, p. 3 of 3, on 4/29/2007.

177   See Appendix, Item 3, p. 126.

178   Ibid.

179   Ibid.

180   Weapons of the American Revolution - Artillery, http://www.americanrevolution.org/artillery.html, pp. 8 and 9 of 37, on 4/16/2008.

James Lambert personally witnessed the effective use of a swivel gun when a cannon ball literally split open a war medic attending to a fallen soldier on the Cowpens battlefield. It is my speculation that what James Lambert witnessed was the effective use of a swivel cannon by the American forces against the British war medic over his fallen British soldier. It is important to note that few swivel cannons were available for use at the Cowpens battlefield. In addition, James Lambert was wounded in his leg and he carried the scar for rest of his life. From the specific testimony given by James Lambert with respect to these personal experiences, one can only conclude that James Lambert was engaged in the Battle of Cowpens. It is understandable that these experiences were so horrific that the visual images stayed with James Lambert for over 63 years, and he was age 86 at the time he testified under oath.

The following information on the Battle of Cowpens, 17 January 1781, was obtained from the American Revolution History Archives, sponsored by the Sons of the American Revolution.

"General Nathaniel Greene took command of the Southern Army of the United States on December 2, 1780, at Charlotte, North Carolina. Although he found few forces to command, on arrival, the American victory at King's Mountain in October had its effect and with the assistance of his commanders he soon organized a substantial army. Foremost among them was General Daniel Morgan, of Virginia, who had fought with Montgomery at Quebec and with Gates at Saratoga, an outstanding leader of distinction. General Morgan was a well educated, but tough, vigorous and hardy product of the frontier, having earned his title of 'The Old Wagoner' through long years of guiding parties of settlers, traders and Indian fighters in their wagon trains. He knew how to lead the frontier militiamen and inspire them to hold their ground and do their best under adverse conditions in the face of well-trained, seasoned British Regular troops. His portraits show him in the buckskins of the frontier. General Greene had appointed General Morgan to command the 'light infantry.'

The campaign in North Carolina might well be described as 'The River Campaign' because the movements of troops on both sides were often determined by the many broad, deep and swift rivers in the area, flowing generally southeasterly toward the coast. Greene's foresight in providing for the construction and transport in wagons of flatboats from one river to another, proved to be of the utmost importance in the campaign. The rivers were the Broad,

Pacolet, Catawba, Dan, Enoree, Tiger, Deep, Haw, Santee, Congaree, Cape Fear and others, including several large creeks and tributaries.

On December 16, Greene directed Morgan to cross the Catawba to its western side, join the North Carolina Militia under General William Davidson, and operate between the Broad and Pacolet Rivers 'either offensively or defensively, as your own prudence and discretion may direct - acting with caution and avoiding surprises by every possible precaution.' The main objectives of Morgan were to protect the people, to annoy the enemy, and to collect and store provisions and forage. If Cornwallis attacked Greene's other force, at Cheraw Hill, Morgan was to rejoin and support that force.

On January 2, Lord Cornwallis ordered Colonel Banastre Tarleton to leave Ninety-Six and push Morgan to the utmost, either destroy Morgan's troops or push them across the Broad River towards Kings Mountain. Tarleton had about 1,100 troops, well-trained regular soldiers for the most part, including his own cavalry known as 'Tarleton's Legion,' a battalion of the Royal Fusiliers, a battalion of the 71st Highland Regiment, a party of Light Dragoons and a detachment of the Royal Artillery, with two light cannon. Morgan's corps consisted of 320 Continentals, 200 Virginia riflemen, 80 of Lt. Colonel William Washington's dragoons, and the remainder were North Carolina, South Carolina and Georgia militiamen, making a total of about 1,040 troops. But in trained regulars Tarleton outnumbered Morgan more than three to one.

As Tarleton's troops approached, General Morgan withdrew to a place called 'The Cowpens' where a local farmer penned his cattle. Today, it is located near Interstate Highway 85, between Kings Mountain National Military Park and Spartanburg, about three hours drive from Atlanta.

Morgan's choice of a battlefield has been severely criticized because it offered no protection from Tarleton's superior cavalry and trained regular troops. Lt. Colonel Henry Lee of Virginia, the famous 'Light Horse Harry,' father of General Robert E. Lee, had been sent by the Commander of Chief to join Greene's forces in the South, although he was not with Morgan at Cowpens. Colonel Lee later pointed out that beyond the Broad River, near Kings Mountain, there was a much better position which Morgan could have taken for the battle, but Morgan stoutly defended his position:

'I would not have had a swamp in view of my militia on any consideration; they would have made for it, and nothing could have detained them from it . . . I knew my adversary, and was perfectly sure I should have nothing but downright fighting. As to retreat, it was the very thing I wished to cut off all hope of . . . When men are forced to fight, they will sell their lives dearly and I knew that the dread of Tarleton's cavalry would give due weight to the protection of my bayonets and keep my troops from breaking . . . Had I crossed the river, one half of my militia would have immediately abandoned me.'

It was undoubtedly also a factor that Morgan, a fighter by nature, was irked by being obliged to withdraw before the oncoming Tarleton, and turned on his foe because he wanted to give battle, disregarding the weakness of his position. But whatever may be said of his choice of the battleground, there is no criticism of the disposition of his troops. It was novel, ingenious and masterly. The evening before the battle, Morgan, true to his frontier background and innate skill as a 'leader of men' visited the campfires, talking and joking with his men in their own language, his voice cheerful, and his manner confident and reassuring. He told them that 'the Old Wagoner' would crack the whip over Ban Tarleton in the morning as sure as he lived. 'Just hold up your heads, boys; give them two fires and you're free.' They had a good night's rest and a full breakfast the next morning. After breakfast, Morgan formed his battle line. He placed his most dependable Continental troops, with seasoned militia, in his main line with Colonel John Eager Howard of Maryland in command. About one hundred fifty yards in front, there were 300 militiamen under Colonel Pickens of South Carolina in a line three hundred yards long. In front of them, in a similar line, were 150 picked riflemen, as sharpshooters. Back of all the infantry and concealed by high ground and trees were William Washington's dragoons and a detachment of Lt. Colonel James McCall's Georgia mounted infantry, armed with sabers to operate as cavalry.

The sharpshooters in the front line in irregular formation were to take cover behind trees, hold their fire until the enemy was within fifty yards, then take careful aim at the officers and fire two volleys. Then they were to retire slowly, firing at will, and pass through the spaces between the men in the second line of militia, reinforcing it. The second line, thus reinforced, was to fire 'low and deliberately' and when hard pressed by the oncoming British was to retire in good order around the main formation of troops, which lay in wait over a slight rise, concealed from the enemy. There they were to rally, reform and act as reserve troops.

The orders were not given to the officers only, but every man was informed of the plan of action and all those in the second line were especially cautioned not to be alarmed by the falling back and apparent defeat of the men in front of them. All of the militia men in the first two lines were mounted and their horses were tied to trees behind the cavalry reserve, an arrangement very consoling to their owners as affording a means of swift retreat in case of disaster. This disposition having been made, the men were told to sit down and rest until the enemy was sighted, but not break formation. Morgan then rode along the lines, encouraging the men in his confident and assured manner. As a result of his leadership, planning and foresight, the men were in good spirits and ready for a fight.

On the British side, the flamboyant Tarleton, eager to fulfill his promise to destroy Morgan's corps or push them back towards Kings Mountain, where Cornwallis would finish them off, had allowed his men little rest that night. At 3:00 o'clock in the morning they were afoot and for five hours thereafter, mostly in the dark, they marched on muddy roads, through swamps and creeks and over broken ground, covering eight very long miles, before they came in sight of the Americans. When he saw the first line of troops, but without sufficient reconnoitering to observe the main battle line in the rear, he at once ordered his legion cavalry forward to attack the riflemen.

As they came on, they received a volley that emptied fifteen saddles. His famous legion then recoiled, so convinced of the marksmanship of the riflemen that they could not be induced to charge again. The front line riflemen, still firing at will, then retired and took their places in the second line. Tarleton then deployed his troops in battle formation, with his two field pieces deployed for action and immediately ordered his whole line forward. The second line of the Americans, under Colonel Pickens of South Carolina, waited until the enemy were 'within killing distance.' Then, taking careful aim with their rifles, they delivered their fire, reloaded and fired again with deadly accuracy, resulting in many casualties.

Although the British line wavered, it continued moving forward and Pickens' men, according to orders, turned about and ran toward the rear of the main American battle line, pursued by the mounted British dragoons. To their astonishment, the mounted troops of Washington and McCall, until that time out of sight, charged forward, swords in hand, on the rear of the attacking dragoons and routed them completely. Pickens' troops gained the safety of the rear lines.

As Morgan had anticipated, retreat of the first two lines of troops was mistaken by Tarleton for the flight of the entire army. Giving their traditional loud battle cries, they rushed forward with fixed bayonets only to be met with another unwavering and deadly fire from the main battle line of Continental soldiers and seasoned militia. The equally courageous British line came on relentlessly and there was hot fighting for nearly half an hour. Another American withdrawal became necessary because Tarleton had called on his reserve of Highlanders and they were about to outflank the American line. As Tarleton saw this second withdrawal, he ordered up his cavalry and the rest of his force. His men, eager to outstrip the others, broke ranks and charged forward towards the Americans in total disorder. Colonel Washington, noticing the confusion, sent word to Morgan. 'They are coming on like a mob. Give them one fire and I'll charge them.'

Just as Pickens' riflemen, having made a complete circuit of the field, came up on Morgan's right as reinforcements. Morgan gave the order 'Face about, give them one fire and the day is ours!' The oncoming British line was charging in a mad rush forward over the hill and were within fifty yards of their enemy when Morgan's order was obeyed. The whole American line blazed with gunfire. The shock was terrific. Colonel Howard, one of the outstanding commanders of the war, saw the moment for the final order, 'Give them the bayonet!' As the seasoned Continental troops, reinforced by the militia, charged into the disorganized British ranks, the mounted infantry and cavalry of Washington and McCall struck them on the flank and in the rear. With bayonet and saber, they split the disorganized Redcoats and tore them apart.

Although the battle in the center was over, on the American right, the 71st Highlanders held out and the British dragoons on the left were still active. Pickens' riflemen attacked the dragoons with such destructive fire that they fled the field, but the Highlanders fought on. Not until the whole weight of the American forces fell upon them were they forced to yield and their commander, Major McArthur, gave up his sword to Colonel Pickens.

Tarleton urged his reserve of 200 dragoons to go forward, but they refused to move. He then tried to protect and remove his two artillery pieces, but Washington again attacked and drove the remaining British troops from the field, except for the artillerymen who stuck to their guns. They were the last to be overcome and never did surrender. Almost to a man, they were struck down at their posts. Washington followed Tarleton who was in full retreat and got well ahead of his own troops.

Seeing that, Tarleton and two of his officers turned and attacked him. One of them aimed his saber at Washington, but an American sergeant, who had caught up with his commander, caught the blow on his own saber. Another British officer was about to cut down Washington when a fourteen-year-old black bugler shot him with his pistol. Tarleton himself made a saber thrust at the American colonel but the blow was parried, he fired his pistol, wounding Washington's horse and then galloped away. This episode has been portrayed in a famous painting which may be seen at Page 230. 'The American Heritage Book of the Revolution.'

The victory was complete, with nearly nine-tenths of the British force killed or captured, with 800 muskets, 35 baggage wagons, 100 dragoon horses, a large quantity of ammunition, and the colors of the 7th Regiment. Congress reacted with resolutions for 'a complete and important victory,' promotions, swords, medals and other rewards.

The battle again proved the value of militia when properly handled by competent leaders and it gave a deathblow to Tarleton's reputation as a military leader. Today, a magnificent portrait of Colonel Tarleton, in complete military uniform with black-plumed helmet and jackboots, may be seen in the British National Portrait Gallery in London.

But there were far more important results of the battle. In the opinion of John Marshall, 'Seldom has a battle, in which greater numbers were not engaged, been so important in its consequences as that of Cowpens.' It gave General Greene his chance to conduct a campaign of 'dazzling shiftiness' that led Cornwallis by 'an unbroken chain of consequences to the catastrophe at Yorktown which finally separated America from the British crown.'"[181]

There is a map that shows the initial British attack at the Battle of Cowpens, South Carolina, on the morning of 17 January 1781.[182]

On January 14th, 2006, more than 2,000 people assembled on a farm just northeast of the Cowpens National Battlefield Park, South Carolina, to participate in (whether as reenactors or spectators) the 225th Anniversary Reenactment of the Battle of Cowpens. It was a cold and windy day, but the sun was shining brightly if not warmly. It was an impressive event and pictures of this event appeared on the web site sponsored by the North Carolina Society of the Sons of the American Revolution.

One of the pictures (Photo 55) was of a reenactor of some repute; namely, Jeff Lambert, Bethabara Chapter, NCSSAR, Immediate Past President.[183]

It is my informed opinion that James Lambert served under the following leaders at the time of the Battle of Cowpens:

General Nathanael Greene, Brigadier General Daniel Morgan and Colonel John Eager Howard.

I think it is most likely that James Lambert was placed in the main battle line of Morgan's most dependable Continental troops, with seasoned militia, under the command of Colonel Howard of Maryland.

"Morgan's plan of battle was to use the Maryland Continentals and the Virginia Militia (of worth equal to the Continentals, as many had served in preview (previous) campaigns) in his main position on the summit of the southernmost ridge and astride the Mill Gap Road. . . .

---

181   The Real Story of the American Revolution - Cowpens, Sponsored by the Sons of the American Revolution, http://www.rsar.org/military/gacowpen.htm, pp. 1-6 of 6, on 4/17/2008.

182   Map of the Battle of Cowpens, South Carolina, http://images.military.com, p. 1 of 1, on 5/13/2008.

183   Cowpens Reenactment 2006, http://www.ncssar.com/images/ CowpensReenactment2006/index.htm, p. 1 of 1, on 11/22/2006.

At this time Howard's Maryland and Delaware Continentals consisted of 237 men. They were placed on the left of the line, astride the Mill Gap Road. To their right were Captain Beate's and Major Triplett's companies of Virginia Militia, under the command of the latter, and totaling about 100 men. Captains Tate and Buchanan with about 100 of the Augusta riflemen of Virginia, supported the right of the line."[184]

According to the testimony of James Lambert under oath, the officers he served under in the Southern Department during his fourth tour of duty included General Greene, Colonel Morgan and Colonel Howard.[185]

It is possible that James Lambert was one of the 150 picked riflemen, as sharpshooters, in the front line who held their fire until the enemy was within fifty yards, taking careful aim at the officers and firing two volleys before retiring slowly to the second line of militia. Of course, the front line and the second line both fell back to the main battle line, being under the same military leadership; namely, General Morgan and Colonel Howard.

Further factors that justify one to conclude that James Lambert was an active participant in the Battle of Cowpens are the following personal and unique observations and experiences he reported:

(1) He saw an iron ball from a swivel cannon split open a war medic attempting to aid a fallen British soldier. The use of a swivel cannon in this field of battle was rare and only a witness could make such a graphic and accurate report of this incident;

(2) His messmate, Thomas Warmsley (Wamsley), had the straps of his knapsack shot off; and

(3) He was personally struck by a musket ball that left a scar in his leg for the rest of his life.

Battle of Guilford Court House, North Carolina, on 15 March 1781

"From the Cowpens, we marched with the prisoners there taken about 300 in number for Virginia and it was understood that Lord Cornwallis was in pursuit of the forces under the command of Morgan. He joined the main army under Genl Greene near a river called Bannister River and marched direct for Guilford, N.C. It was some time after this before the Battle of Guilford was fought as much as two or three weeks. Here he was marched and counter marched for some days in hearing of the enemy until in March

---

184   The Battle of Cowpens, Part III, Deployment of Troops–The Battle, http://www. newrivernotes.com/misc/cowpens1.htm, pp. 8 and 9 of 14, on 4/17/2008.

185   See Appendix, Item 3, p. 127.

1781 *(the day he does not remember) the Battle was fought. Here the enemy kept the field but immediately retreated, leaving some of their wounded. The enemy marched for their shipping at Wilmington."*[186]

The Banister River is a tributary of the Dan River, about 65 miles long, in southern Virginia. It rises on Brier Mountain in western Pittsylvania County and flows generally eastwardly into Halifax County, past the town of Halifax. It joins the Dan River 6 miles east of the town of South Boston.[187]

The following information on the Battle of Guilford Court House, 15 March 1781, was also obtained from the American Revolution History Archives, sponsored by the Sons of the American Revolution.

"After the victory at Cowpens, Morgan did not rest on his laurels. Cornwallis' much greater army was nearby and poised to cut off Morgan's retreat in the event of the expected British victory. Now, he was ready to attack Morgan's force, victorious, but weakened by the battle. Between Morgan and Greene were four rivers, the Broad, the Catawba, Lynch's Creek and the Pee Dee. Cornwallis marched north to attack Morgan, but Morgan took the road to Ramsour's Mills,-northeastward, and passed that crossroads on January 23, having crossed the Broad and the Catawba Rivers and putting them between his troops and the pursuing British. Morgan had covered one hundred miles in less than five days, crossing two rivers in the journey under very difficult conditions.

In an effort to catch the fast moving Americans, Cornwallis made a momentous decision. He spent two days destroying most of his baggage, wagons, tents and surplus provisions. At this time, seeing the supplies destroyed, many Hessian troops and some British soldiers deserted, perhaps as many as 250. The decision of Cornwallis to lighten his baggage in an effort to catch the enemy, was a magnificent gesture, but in the end it proved to be 'vain and useless and finally fatal' to Cornwallis and his army.

On January 25, General Greene, encamped at Cheraw, received news of the victory at Cowpens, took measures to assist Morgan and prepared to move his forces with Morgan's across the Dan River into Virginia, where American reinforcements in large numbers were expected. He ordered boats to be assembled on the Dan River at the boundary between North Carolina and Virginia. Greene then rode with a small detachment the one hundred twenty-five miles to confer with Morgan at his camp on the Catawba. When Greene

---

186   Ibid., pp. 126 and 127.

187   Banister River - Wikipedia, the free encyclopedia, http://en.wikipedia.org/wiki/ Banister_River, p. 1 of 1 on 4/19/2008.

learned that Cornwallis had destroyed most of his supplies and equipment, he conceived a plan to lead Cornwallis north, farther and farther from his supply bases on the coast, while drawing nearer and nearer to his own in Virginia and the North. Morgan opposed the plan as dangerous, but Greene decided on it and overruled Morgan's objections.

Thereafter followed the famous Retreat to the Dan, 'one of the most memorable in the annals of war.' Only about 2,000 in the American Army and less than 3,000 British were engaged, but its consequences were great and it led, finally, to entrapment of the British army at Yorktown. The American forces reached the Dan River first and safely crossed, thanks to the prudent advance preparations made. The rear guard, 'Light Horse Harry' Lee's cavalry, reached the boats at the river and safely crossed just before the advancing British troops arrived. The river was too high to cross without boats and every boat was on the farther shore in the hands of the Americans. Greene had won the race.

When Greene crossed into Virginia, it left the British forces in complete domination of Georgia, South Carolina and North Carolina, including the only major ports: Charleston and Savannah. Cornwallis issued a proclamation calling all citizens to join him 'with their weapons and ten days provisions.'

But wars are not fought nor victories won by stationary armies and stable conditions. Although the expected reinforcements from Virginia drifted slowly to the American army, Greene decided to return to North Carolina and give the forces of Cornwallis the battle they had been seeking. Six weeks before, on his way north, Greene had passed through the area where he now determined to make his stand. On April (March) 14, he went into camp near Guilford Court House. Today, the battlefield, a National Military Park, lies just north of the City of Greensboro, North Carolina. On the day of encampment, Greene's forces consisted of 4,400 men, many of them never before battle tested and many of the militia unreliable. But it was as large an army as was ever assembled in the South up to that time and it greatly outnumbered Cornwallis' army, probably about 1,900.

When Greene marched to Guilford, Cornwallis was encamped at New Garden, about twelve miles southwest and Greene's move was a challenge which Cornwallis could neither ignore nor refuse. In fact, it gave him the opportunity he had been seeking for two months. And scarcity of supplies (due in large part to his own destruction of them) now compelled him either to fight or retreat toward the seacoast. As between those alternatives, Lord Cornwallis, an honorable, brave and courageous soldier who never fled a good fight, did not hesitate.

Greene sent Lee's legion with a detachment of riflemen toward the British encampment at New Garden. Three or four miles from Guilford, Lee met Tarleton leading the oncoming

British forces. A hot skirmish followed before Lee 'retired precipitately' to notify Greene of the oncoming Redcoats.

Not long before, Daniel Morgan, from his home in Virginia, a casualty of arthritis and rheumatism, had written to Greene with wise advice about the American militia. 'If they fight, you beat Cornwallis. If not, he will beat you.' He advised flanking the lines of militia with riflemen under good officers. 'Put the . . . militia in the center with some fixed troops in their rear to shoot down the first man that runs.'

Greene followed Morgan's advice. He fixed his lines in front of the Court House, perched upon high ground, with split rail fence in front, woods on the flanks and an open field of five hundred yards which the British would have to cross to reach the line behind the fence. His artillery centered on the road to the Court House. The cavalry of Lee and Washington was placed on either flank of the forward line with the Virginia and Maryland Continental troops on the high ground in the rear. Greene followed Morgan's example in dealing with the militia and walked along the lines asking as Morgan had done before Cowpens for two volleys before they retired. 'Two rounds, my boys, and then you may fall back.'

About half past one, the battle began with the advance of the British center into the clearing, fifes playing and drums beating. After they had crossed more than two- thirds of the open field, the first volley of 1,000 rifles spoke and gaps appeared in the advancing scarlet line, but it came steadily forward. Within one hundred yards of the rail fence, the line halted, delivered a volley and bravely charged forward, but it halted again some fifty yards from the fence because, wrote Sergeant Lamb of the Welch Fusiliers, it was seen that the American forces had their arms resting on a rail fence, aiming with nice precision.

As the troops watched each other, face to face, Colonel Webster of the Fusiliers, rode forward and shouted, 'Come on, my brave Fusiliers.' They rushed forward and into the teeth of the enemy's fire with dreadful havoc on both sides. The North Carolina militia had now delivered their two fires as ordered. There was no time to reload, even if they tried and without a moment's hesitation, they turned and ran back through the woods, and the second line, to safety. They had done what they had been asked to do and they had the commander's permission to leave the field. The British were now up to the second fence with no opponent visible, but there was a steady fire upon both their flanks, so they wheeled to the left and right to meet the challenge, the Grenadiers and the 2nd battalion of Guards assuming the position in the center.

Cornwallis held the field. He had a victory, but he had paid a price. Of 1,900 men who went into battle on the British side, more than a fourth were casualties, 93 dead and 439 wounded. The clear ground was behind and the fighting now was from tree to tree, hand *to hand, with much heroism on both sides. There was cavalry attack and counter attack; the troops became mixed together and Cornwallis finally ordered the artillery to fire grape shot into the melee of British and American troops, forcing the Americans to withdraw and allowing the British a chance to re-form. At the end, a general retreat took place by the Americans, 'but it was conducted with order and regularity' wrote Seedman, an English historian who was in the battle . . . heavy casualties among the officers. Not counting the militia who ran clear away and were reported 'missing,' Greene's casualties were 78 killed and 183 wounded.*

In this battle, on both sides, the most admirable military qualities were displayed. All gave proof of a high degree of valor and steadfastness. On the whole, however, the laurels for military achievement must be awarded to the British. Starting hungry, they marched twelve hard miles and immediately went into battle against an enemy of greater numbers (disregarding the North Carolina militia there were more than 3,000 Americans against 1,900 British) who had been refreshed by a night's sleep and breakfast. That enemy force was so posted as to have every advantage of its skill in woodcraft and marksmanship and the superiority of the rifle over the musket.

But the British faltered not at all in advancing across a quarter-mile of open ground against two rifle volleys precisely aimed. When the 33rd and the Guards were shattered, the Guards, indeed, torn to pieces, they rallied, re-formed, and attacked with no less vigor for their punishment. Fortescue, the historian of the British army, surveying its whole history from Crecy and Agincourt to the middle of the nineteenth century, says, 'Never, perhaps, has the prowess of the British soldier been seen to greater advantage than in this obstinate and bloody combat.' The merits and achievements of the Americans in this battle are enhanced, in the judgment of history, in proportion to the military ability of those opponents."[188]

The following gives a good description of the three American lines of troops:

"Green's troops were drawn up in three lines, approximately 400 yards apart, facing west. The first two lines extended north and south across the New Garden road, the third line was entirely north of the road, following the crest of a low hill. Heavily wooded terrain limited the effectiveness of cavalry. The woods likewise reduced the effectiveness of artillery since the field of fire, particularly for the attacking force, was poor. Approximately one-half mile in front of the position, was a small stream from which the ground rose steadily, though rather gradually, to the crest of a hill where the first line was drawn up. Three cultivated

---

188   The Real Story of the American Revolution – Guilford, Sponsored by the Sons of the American Revolution, http://www.rsar.org/military/gaguilfo.htm, pp. 1-4 of 4, on 3/19/2007.

fields, one to the north and two to the south of the road, provided an excellent field of fire for parts of the line, and the rail fences enclosing the cultivated land afforded the troops some protection. The second line was entirely in the woods, and the third was near the eastern edge of a good-sized clearing.

Both flanks of the first two lines and the right flank of the third were unprotected. But the heavy woods dictated a direct frontal attack by the British; therefore these exposed flanks were not a disadvantage for the Americans. The left flank of the third line rested on the New Garden Road and was protected by artillery during the later stages of the battle.

The First Line consisted of two brigades of North Carolina Militia, almost all of whom were wholly untrained and entirely without battle experience. On the left flank were stationed Lt. Col. Henry Lee's Legion and Col. William Campbell's Riflemen. The former were regulars and the latter were frontiersmen from the Virginia and North Carolina mountains who had had appreciable campaign experience, including participation in the Battle of Kings Mountain. The right flank detachment was composed of Lt. Col. William Washington's regular cavalry, the remnant of the Delaware regiment of Continentals, and Col. Charles Lynch's Riflemen, comparable in experience and capacity to Campbell's. In the center on the road, a section of artillery, two 6-pound guns, commanded the stream-crossing below.

The Second Line was made up entirely of Virginia Militia, the majority of whom were as untrained and inexperienced as were the North Carolinians in the front line. The Virginia officers, however, were largely men who had served in the Continental Army, and a number of them had had some battle experience. Also in the ranks of the Virginians were a few men who had had previous military service. Thus the second line was somewhat stronger than the first by virtue of this leaven (level) of experience. Finally, Brig. Gen. Edward Stevens, in command of one brigade, placed sentinels a few yards in the rear of his line to insure against any break by his men.

The Third Line was composed of Greene's two small brigades of Continental troops. Of the four regiments, one the 1ˢᵗ Maryland, was a veteran unit. The 2d Maryland and the two Virginia regiments were recently reorganized, had excellent officers, and contained a good proportion of veterans in the ranks. The total force, regular and militia, infantry, cavalry, and artillery, numbered about 4,400. Of this total possibly 1,500 to 1,600 of all arms were regulars but many of these fell into the recruit classification."[189]

The three lines of the American troops are shown on a map of the Battle of Guilford Court House, 15 March 1781.[190]

189   Guilford Courthouse National Military Park, http://statelibrary.dcr.state.nc.us/nc/ ncsites/greensbo/guilf1.htm, pp. 4 and 5 of 6, on 4/20/2008.

190   Map of the Battle of Guilford Court House, North Carolina, http://www. myrevolutionarywar.com, p. 1 of 1, on 4/19/2008.

The American Forces at Guilford Court House were under the command of Major-General Nathanael Greene and the second in command was Brig. General Isaac Huger. The Continentals included the Maryland Brigade under the leadership of Otho H. Williams and part of that Brigade was the 1st Maryland Regiment under the command of Colonel John Gunby and Lieut. Colonel John Eager Howard. The Virginia Militia included the First Virginia brigade under the leadership of Brig. Gen. Edward Stevens which was composed in considerable part of men from the western Virginia "rifle counties": Rockbridge, Augusta, Rockingham, and perhaps others. Their officers and many in the ranks were experienced soldiers who had fought in earlier campaigns, mostly against Indians.[191]

Lynch's Virginia Rifle Corps of about 360 men were under the leadership of Colonel Charles Lynch. He had brought them down from Bedford County and all but 60 were armed with rifles.[192]

James Lambert made specific reference to Brigadier-General Stevens, including the fact that he was wounded at the Battle of Guilford Courthouse. The very next officer he remembered was Colonel Lynch. James Lambert also remembered General Greene, Colonel Howard, Colonel Lee, Colonel Washington, Colonel Williams and others.[193]

Based upon the recorded recollections of James Lambert and an analysis of the facts about the Battle of Guilford Courthouse, it seems logical to conclude that James Lambert, being an experienced soldier from Augusta County who had fought at Point Pleasant, Great Bridge and Cowpens, was a member of the First Virginia Brigade in the American Third Line under the leadership of Brigadier-General Edward Stevens.

It is possible that James Lambert, being an experienced expert rifleman, was with the Virginia Rifle Corps under the leadership of Colonel Charles Lynch; however, James Lambert was already in the area with Generals Morgan and Greene and he would

---

191   The Battle of Guilford Courthouse, http://www.myrevolutionarywar.com/
        battles/810315.htm, pp. 5 and 6 of 9, on 4/18/2008.

192   Ibid., p. 6.

193   See Appendix, Item 3, pp. 124, 125, 127 and 129.

not have been one of the riflemen Colonel Lynch brought to the area from Bedford County a short time before the battle.

"The Battle of Guilford Court House was not only one of the hardest fought and most deadly conflicts of the American Revolution-creating a profound impression in Europe; but was the decisive engagement of the Southern campaign, contributing no small part to bringing about, almost immediately, the freedom of the Thirteen Colonies."[194]

"The Virginian militia, being hard pressed on their center and left, after Webster had prevailed on their right, gave way altogether, when General Stevens, a great, animating leader in their ranks, received a ball in his right thigh."[195]

"The retreat began near 3:30 in the afternoon, the battle lasting an hour and a half by Cornwallis' watch. . . . Since the horses were killed, Greene was obliged to leave his four field pieces and two ammunition wagons, like the honors of the field, behind him. Lossing says two of those pieces of artillery were taken from Burgoyne at Saratoga; lost by Gates at Camden; retaken by the Americans at Cowpens; and lost again to the British on the field at Guilford. He states, too, that they were of the small variety called 'Grasshoppers.'"[196]

Cornwallis reported that the British had 93 killed and 413 wounded. The American killed and wounded could never be ascertained with any degree of precision; however, it was reported that the First Virginia brigade had 11 killed, 35 wounded and 141 missing.[197]

The following information about the weapons used in the Revolutionary War will enable one to better understand the activities of the soldiers in the Battle of Guilford Court House:

"The flintlock musket was the most important weapon of the Revolutionary War. It represented the most advanced technological weapon of the 18th century. Muskets were smooth-bored, single-shot, muzzle-loading weapons. The standard rate of fire for infantrymen was three shots per minute. The rifle, although slower to load, was more accurate than the musket. However, riflemen were at great disadvantage in close-quarters fighting against

---

194   The Battle of Guilford Court House, http://www.newrivernotes.com/nc/guilf1.htm, p. 1 of 8, on 2/10/2007.
195   Ibid., p. 6.
196   Ibid., p. 7.
197   The Battle of Guilford Courthouse, http://www.myrevolutionarywar.com/battles/810315.htm, pp. 6 and 7 of 9, on 4/18/2008.

disciplined infantry armed with muskets and bayonets. Cavalrymen and officers used pistols. Pistols were effective only at close range.

Edged weapons played a critical role in the Revolutionary War. Battles like Guilford Courthouse were decided in bloody hand-to-hand combat where bayonets, swords, and axes were used.

Riflemen, having no bayonets, relied on knives and tomahawks. Swords were widely used during the war. Infantrymen used hangers, while their officers carried short sabers. Officers' small swords were light, straight, and slender. Hunting swords were short, cut-and-thrust weapons used by the German-Jaegers, American riflemen, and officers of both sides. Pole arms served both as combat weapons and symbols of rank. The bayonet was the most widely used edged weapon of the war. It transformed the musket into a spear. It was a terrifyingly effective weapon when used by an experienced soldier. Inexperienced troops often fled in the face of bayonet charges."[198]

"The two forces met head-on at the Battle of Guilford Courthouse on 15 March 1781. Cornwallis succeeded in driving Greene from the field, but he suffered severe casualties in a Pyrrhic victory. When the British Parliament learned of the battle, Charles James Fox exclaimed, 'Another such victory would destroy the British Army.' Weakened, Cornwallis withdrew to Wilmington, North Carolina and eventually on to Yorktown, Virginia, where he was defeated by a joint Franco-American force."[199]

Next, Greene led his army back into South Carolina and led his main army in three more engagements, the Battle of Hobkirk's Hill (25 April 1781), the Siege of Ninety-Six (22 May-19 June 1781), and the Battle of Eutaw Springs (8 September 1781). A major factor in Greene's success was an outstanding group of subordinates including: two Marylanders, Otho Holland Williams and John Eager Howard, two cavalrymen, William Washington (second cousin of George Washington) and Henry Lee (father of General Robert E. Lee), and his Polish engineer, Thaddeus Kosciusko. After the war, Greene moved his family to his new estate, Mulberry Grove, just north of Savannah, Georgia. He attempted to settle down to the life of a Southern planter, while spurning attempts by prominent Georgians to involve him in local politics. He was forced to

---

198   NPS Museum Collections 'American Revolutionary War: Guilford Courthouse', http:// www.cr.nps.gov/museum/exhibits/revwar/guco/gucoweapons.html, pp. 1 and 2 of 2, on 4/28/2007.

199   Biography of Nathanael Greene, http://members.aol.com/JonMaltbie/Biography.html, p. 4 of 4, on 4/28/2007.

sell additional property awarded to him by the states of North and South Carolina in order to solve severe financial problems caused by the war. Tragically, Greene died at the age of forty-four on 19 June 1786 of a stroke, possibly caused by overexposure to the sun. His remains and those of his son, George Washington Greene, rest beneath a monument in Johnson Square in downtown, Savannah, Georgia. Eventually, Congress would pay off his debt and erect a monument to his memory in the nation's capitol. It will never be known to what great heights he would have risen had he lived a longer life.[200]

The important role Thaddeus Kosciusko played in the Southern Campaign is described as follows:

"Early in August, 1780, a few days after Arnold's arrival at West Point, Kosciusko left the Highlands outpost to join General Gates, who have been newly appointed to take command of the Southern Army in the hope that he could turn the tide against the British in the South as he had done in the North, at Saratoga. Washington was reluctant to let Kosciusko go, explaining to Gates that 'I have experienced great satisfaction from his general conduct, and particularly from the attention and zeal with which he prosecuted the Works committed to his charge at West Point.' In the end the commander in chief did give his permission, but before Kosciusko had time to reach the Southern Army, Gates was dealt a crushing defeat at Camden , South Carolina, and was relieved of command.

The news must have weighed heavily on Kosciusko's mind as he travelled south. Certainly the southern campaigns were taking a miserable toll of lives and reputations. Not only were Georgia and South Carolina now in British hands, but the fall of Savannah the year before had claimed the life of Kosciusko's heroic young compatriot Casimir Pulaski, who had been such a gallant leader in the war of resistance against the First Partition of Poland. Now Kosciusko's dear friend General Gates had been disgraced as well. Nevertheless he continued on his southward journey and assumed the duties of chief engineer under Gates's successor, General Nathanael Greene.

In the busy winter months that followed, Kosciusko explored by canoe the Catawba and Pedee (Pee Dee) rivers in the rugged western wilderness of North Carolina, reporting to Greene on the feasibility of using these rivers not only for transport routes for men and supplies but also as possible highways of retreat to the North if such a move became necessary. Then, while Greene set about rebuilding and resupplying the demoralized Southern Army—in a camp chosen by Kosciusko—the chief engineer was put in charge of

---

200   Ibid.

building a fleet of flat-bottomed boats that could be moved by wagon from one river to another. All this gave Greene the mobility he needed when, in January and February, 1781, Britain's General Cornwallis threatened to destroy the entire Southern Army. In one of the greatest episodes of the Revolution, Greene, with Cornwallis pressing hard on his heels, led a barefoot, ragged, and hungry army on a mad dash of two hundred miles across North Carolina and into Virginia. There Kosciusko's boats got the troops across the Dan River just ahead of the enemy, who had neither boats nor supplies with which to continue the pursuit.

The retreat saved the Southern Army, . . ."[201]

James Lambert informed us in his Amended Declaration (13 May 1844), that after the Battle of Guilford Court House:

". . . he was again at Hillsborough, (North Carolina), from thence he marched to Broadford on Adkin River and remained there for some time how long he cannot state but he was there discharged and returned with many men of the Virginia Militia back to their homes. This tour of two years he served out his time in full and was honorably discharged by Col. Hillyard in writing. That discharge has since been lost by being in the possession of one William Bennett who was drowned about one year afterwards."[202]

James Lambert also informed us in the same document that:

"He continued in the service until after the Battle of Guilford when he was discharged in May or June 1781."[203]

There is today a town named Broadford in the southwest corner of Virginia near the borders of North Carolina and Tennessee. There is also a town a few miles east of Broadford named "Atkins."[204]

Although I have not been able to find a river named either "Atkin" or "Atkins," I did find the following information about the Middle Fork Holston River:

"The headwaters of the Middle Fork Holston River are located near the Smyth-Wythe County line in Southwest Virginia. The river flows approximately 56 miles through Smyth and Washington counties and connects with the South Fork Holston River to form South

---

201   American Heritage.com/Kosciusko, http://www.americanheritage.com, p. 6 of 10, on 3/18/2008.

202   See Appendix, Item 3, p. 127.

203   Ibid., p. 125.

204   Map of Broadford and Atkins, Virginia, by MapQuest, http://www.mapquest.com, p. 1 of 2, on 4/24/2008.

Holston Reservoir. The river has many different sport fish species for all types of anglers. In the upper sections of the river near the towns of Atkins and Marion there are two designated stocked trout areas. Near the town of Atkins there is a Class 'B' stocked trout section that is stocked five times from October through May. . . ."[205]

It is reasonable to assume that this was the general area in Virginia where James Lambert spent most of his time in the last few months of his fourth tour of military duty.

However, James Lambert also told us the following:

"He will mention one thing more, when he was in Richmond he saw the Americans using a diving bell to recover the Brass Canon (Cannon) which the British had sunk said to be "Sixty."[206]

My further research has found that Virginia navy vessels, numbering nine larger vessels and an unknown number of smaller vessels, were anchored near Osbornes on 27 April 1781. Osbornes was then a small port village on the south side of the James River at the mouth of Proctors Creek approximately fifteen miles southeast of Richmond, Virginia. Benedict Arnold and his British land troops were able to either sink or capture the nine larger vessels; namely, the Tempest (20 guns), Jefferson (14 guns), Renown (26 guns), Apollo (18 guns), Willing Lass (12 guns), Wilkes (12 guns), Mars (8guns), American Fabious (18 guns) and Morning Star (12 guns). It is interesting to note that if the Tempest, Jefferson and Renown were sunk there would be a total of 60 brass cannon guns in the James River for the Americans to recover. There is no clear record of what happened to the ships of the Virginia navy. There was a sonar and magnetometer search in 1985 but the team's search produced no conclusive results and their report stated that;

"We found no trace of the Virginia Navy shipwrecks. No targets of any consequence turned up on the side scan sonar or magnetometer. . . . the river has moved west in the past 200 years and if the colonials did not raise the wrecks after the war, their remains lie buried in the marsh northeast and under the land of Farrar Island."[207]

---

205   Fishing Getaways - Virginia Mountains - Smyth County, Virginia, http://www. visitvirginiamountains.com/fishing.html, p. 1 of 2, on 4/24/2008.

206   See Appendix, Item 3, p. 127.

207   Darley, Stephen F., <u>The Battle of Osbornes on the James River</u>, Southern Campaigns of the American Revolution, April 2006, Vol. 3 No. 4.0, p. 40, http://www.southerncampaign.org., on 4/24/2008.

The American regulars of Major General Lafayette's army arrived at Richmond in time to prevent the British from taking over Richmond, and the British leaders decided that their expedition had been completely successful and ordered their troops to march along the James River back to Portsmouth.[208]

It is interesting to note that James Lambert was in the area of Richmond, Virginia, to personally witness the Americans efforts to recover the sixty brass cannons the British had sunk in the James River on 27 April 1781. It is most likely that James saw these events sometime in May 1781, since he was discharged near Broadford, Virginia, in May or June, 1781.

It is also reported that:

"General Charles Cornwallis occupied the town (Richmond, Virginia) *in June 1781."*[209]

The Richard Bennett Pension File No. W 9350

During my visit to the Allen County Public Library, Fort Wayne, Indiana, in late September 2007, I found and copied portions of the above referenced file, including an Affidavit by James Lambert. This Affidavit was dated and certified by James Dill, Clerk of the Dearborn Circuit Court in Dearborn County, Indiana, on 3 April 1826. James Lambert personally appeared that day before Daniel Hagerman, a Justice of the Peace for Dearborn County, Indiana. One point of interest is the Clerk's certification contained the statement:

"I have hereunto affixed the mutilated seal of our said court (the said seal having been injured by fire on the night of the 5ᵗʰ of March 1826)."[210]

This gives us direct evidence that the two-story frame Dearborn County Court House built in 1810 was destroyed by fire on 5 March 1826.

---

208   City of Petersburg "MAJOR GENERAL WILLIAM PHILLIPS". http://www. petersburg-va.org/revwar/phillips.htm, p. 2 of 3, on 3/24/2007.

209   Henrico County, Virginia, History Highlights, The American Revolution, p. 3.

210   See Appendix, Item 11, p. 140.

James Dill, Clerk of the Dearborn Circuit Court

James Dill, born in Dublin, Ireland, in 1772, came to America shortly after the Revolutionary War and settled in the Northwest Territory, moving to Dearborn County in 1803.[211]

Congress split the Northwest Territory into the Indiana Territory and the Northwest Territory on 7 May 1800. William Henry Harrison was appointed Governor of the Indiana Territory on 13 May 1800.[212]

James Dill was a member of the Indiana territorial House of Representatives (1811-1813) and became its Speaker of the House.[213]

By a 4 to 3 vote, the Indiana General assembly petitioned Congress for statehood on 11 December 1811. Representatives, Peter Jones of Knox, James Dill of Dearborn, and Richard Rue of Wayne opposed the petition and sent their written objections; namely, the territory was too small, population too scattered and cost of state government too expensive. The petition was denied but the congressional committee would allow statehood when the population reached 35,000. Due to the lack of money the territory did not further pursue statehood prior to the War of 1812.[214]

James Dill was a friend of Governor William Henry Harrison and the son-in-law of General Arthur St. Clair.[215] Governor Harrison appointed James Dill as a General

211   Finding Aid from the Manuscript Section of the Indiana State Library, Dill Family Papers, S1819, 1803-1837, processing by Barbara Hilderbrand, May 2007, http://www.statelib.lib.in.us/www/isl/indiana/manuscrips/aids/s1819.html, p. 1 of 2, on 8/12/2008; The Political Graveyard: Index to Politicians: Dilan to Diluglio, http://politicalgraveyard.com/bio/dilas-dills.html, p. 3 of 13, on 8/12/2008; and IHB: Members of Indiana's 1816 Constitutional Convention, http://www.in.gov/history/2952.htm, p. 1 of 5, on 8/14/2008..

212   Indiana Fun Facts 'History', http://www.usstatereports.com/funFacts.aspx?st=IN&type='History', p. 1 of 2, on 8/12/2008.

213   The Political Graveyard:Index to Politicians: Dilan to Diluglio, http://politicalgraveyard.com/bio/dilas-dills.html, p. 3 of 13, on 8/12/2008; and Finding Aid from the Manuscripts Section of the Indiana State Library, Dill Family Papers, S1819, 1803-1837, processing by Barbara Hilderbrand, May 2007, http://www.statelib.lib.in.us/www/isl/indiana/manuscripts/aids/s1819/html, p. 1 of 2, on 8/12/2008.

214   Indiana Fun Facts 'History', http://www.usstatereports.com/funFacts.aspx?st=IN&type='History', p. 1 of 2, on 8/12/2008.

215   Finding Aid from the Manuscript Section of the Indiana State Library, Dill Family Papers, S1819, 1803-1837, processing by Barbara Hilderbrand, May 2007, http://wwwstatelib.lib.in.us/www/isl/indiana/manuscripts/aids/s1819.html, p. 1 of 2, on 8/12/2008.

during the War of 1812.[216] He was also appointed brigadier general of the territorial militia, on 15 January 1816.[217]

The Indiana General Assembly petitioned Congress once again for statehood on 11 December 1815, and President James Monroe signed an Enabling Act to allow the Indiana Territory to hold a constitutional convention. On 10 June 1816, 43 duly elected Constitutional delegates met at the capital, Corydon, to compose Indiana's state constitution. On 11 June 1816, James Dill, delegate and lawyer from Lawrenceburg, reported 27 rules for government of the convention. The Indiana Constitution of 1816 was signed on 29 June 1816, and James Dill was one of the three signers from the County of Dearborn. On 11 December 1816, President James Madison approved Indiana's admission into the union as the 19th state.[218]

James Dill was one of the first members of the bar in Dearborn County and he was the first recorder of Dearborn County. He was also a member of the anti-slavery party. He died in 1838 and is buried somewhere in Lawrenceburg, Indiana.[219]

The town of Dillsborough was laid out in 1830 and the present spelling of Dillsboro was adopted in 1893. It was named for General James Dill, Clerk of the Circuit Court at the time (1830) and a prominent leader in the history of Dearborn County.[220]

---

216   A Brief History of Dearborn County by Chris McHenry, http://www.lpld.lib.in.us/ brief.htm, p. 2 of 6, on 8/12/2008.

217   IHM: Members of Indiana's 1816 Constitutional Convention, http://www.in.gov/ history/2952.htm, p. 1 of 5, on 8/14/2008.

218   Indiana Fun Facts 'History', http://www.usstatereports.com/funFacts.aspx?st=IN&typ e='History', pp. 1 and 2 of 2, on 8/12/2008; and Indiana Constitution of 1816 - wikisource, http://en.wikisource.org/wiki/Indiana_Constitution_of_1816, pp. 16 and 17 of 18, on 8/12/2008.

219   Finding Aid from the Manuscript Section of the Indiana State Library, Dill Family Papers, S1819, 1803-1837, processing by Barbara Hilderbrand, May 2007, http:// www.statelib.lib.in.us/www/isl/indiana/manuscripts/aids/s1819.html, p. 1 of 2, on 8/12/2008; and The Political Graveyard: Index to Politicians: Dilan to Diluglio, http:// politicalgraveyard.com/bio/dilas-dills.html, p. 3 of 13, on 8/12/2008.

220   Historic Southern Indiana, http://www.usi.edu/HSI/trivia/placenames.asp, p. 9 of 18, on 8/12/2008; and Town of Dillsboro, http://www.townofdillsboro.us/, p. 1 of 1, on 8/12/2008.

Affidavit of James Lambert (3 April 1826) Duly Certified by James Dill, Clerk of the Dearborn Circuit Court

In the Affidavit, James Lambert stated the following under oath:

"That Richard Bennett and this deponent enlisted at the same time at Richmond in the State of Virginia during the War under Captain John Slaughter, that they were afterwards attached to the Second Regiment of United States infantry under the command of Col. Guy Hamilton and Brigadier Gen. Rufus Putnam—that they enlisted in the year of 1781—during the war—that they served together in the same ranks until the close of the war, and at that time they were discharged, that afterwards they served a tour of duty as militia men, and were also discharged from those services—and further states that he is perfectly acquainted with the services of Richard Bennett and that he was Honorably discharged and further saith not."[221]

The Original Claim Declaration of Richard Bennett (Bennet), dated 10 April 1826, was certified on 17 April 1826 by Jonathan K. Wilds, Clerk of the Court of Common Pleas within and for the County of Warren and State of Ohio.

Richard Bennett (Bennet) stated that he was 63 years of age, meaning he was born in 1763, and that he enlisted in the Spring of 1781 in Richmond, Virginia. His Company was commanded by Captain John Slaughter in the Regiment commanded by Col. Hamilton of the Virginia Continental Line. He then later served a tour with the Virginia Militia.

As a result of the passage of an Act of Congress on 7 June 1832, Richard Bennett (Bennet) made a reappearance before the Court on 2 October 1832 and stated that he enlisted in the army of the United States at the City of Richmond in Virginia some time in March 1781. He stated further that he was in the company of Captain Hamilton under Colonel Slaughter. He remained in Richmond and the neighborhood guarding public property, stored and otherwise. He was then marched towards little York (former name of Yorktown) but was halted to guard baggage wagons and other property, remaining there until surrender of Lord Cornwallis. Thereafter, recalled to Richmond to guard public property in particular a large number of Negroes,

---

221   See Appendix, Item 11, p. 139.

perhaps seventy, who had been captured from the British. In the Spring of 1782 he and a dozen others of Captain Hamilton's Company were sent to a Fort in Crabapple Bottom, Virginia. Towards the fall of 1782 he was ordered to the Tygart Valley. Late in the fall of 1782 Col. Benjamin Wilson gave him a letter to Col. Moffett near Staunton, Virginia, who then gave him a written discharge, being in the service a full eighteen months.

Richard Bennett (Bennet) further stated that he had proved his services by the depositions of James Lambert and Abram Bennet.

In an additional declaration, dated 16 September 1833, Richard Bennett (Bennet) stated that he was born in Augusta County, now Pendleton County, Virginia, in the month of May (12th or 13th) in the year 1763. He lived there during his whole term of service. He recollects Capt. Hamilton who commanded his company; Col. Slaughter was the commandant of his regiment; General Putnam took command of his regiment after we marched to Richmond; he had procured the affidavits of Abraham Bennet and James Lambert; he believed James Lambert to be dead and the officer who took his affidavit to be out of office.

The Court was satisfied that Abraham Bennet knew James Lambert some 45 or 50 years ago (1788-1783) and that he (James Lambert) was a man of veracity and his oath or declaration seriously made entitled to credit was witness being produced to the Court. The Court concluded that Richard Bennett (Bennet) was a Revolutionary soldier and served as he had stated.

Subsequent correspondence in the year 1857 indicate that Richard Bennett's second wife, Margaret Turvey, was born in 1787 and that they were married about 1826. They raised one son, Abram, born about 1827, and Margaret then lived with him in Lawrence County, Ohio. Richard Bennett apparently died in the early part of 1835.

The file also indicated that Richard Bennett had a nephew, named William, who was born in 1779 and was a resident of Warren County, Ohio, on 11 September 1857.

Further, an Examining Clerk noted on 21 February 1833 that Richard Bennett of Warren County, State of Ohio, was 69 years of age; had enlisted in March 1781 for a term of 1 year and 6 months; was a private under Capt. Hamilton and Col. Slaughter; also a scout and Indian spy under Col. Wilson. *"He once before applied for a pension through Judge Kessling and he proved his service by 2 witnesses-supposed their depositions to be now in the War Dept."*

Notes in the Pension File further state that Richard Bennett was a Private in the Company commanded by Captain Hamilton of the Regiment commanded by Col. Slaughter in the Virginia Line for 18 months. "*Inscribed on the Roll of Ohio at the rate of 60 Dollars 00 Cents per annum commence on the 4ᵗʰ day of March, 1831. Certificate of Pension issued the 9ᵗʰ day of November 1833 and sent to J. K. Wilds, Lebanon, Ohio. Arrears to the 4ᵗʰ of September 1823 (1832) $150. and Semianl. Allowance ending 4 Mar 34 $30., (Total) $180.*"

The Pension File also contains a form which states: "*Margaret Bennett, widow of Richard Bennett, Va, who served in the Revolutionary War, as a Private. Inscribed on the Roll at the rate of 60 dollars 00 cents per annum, to commence on the 3ʳᵈ February, 1853. Certificate of Pension issued 2ⁿᵈ day of Oct. 1857 and sent to J. J. Coombs.*"

The U.S. Pensioners, 1818-1872 Reports for the Cincinnati Pension Office indicate that Margaret Bennett, widow of Richard Bennett, received her $30. semi-annual payments from September 1852 to March 1867.[222]

It seems clear from the analysis of the Richard Bennett Pension File that James Lambert, Richard Bennett and the Pension authorities all agreed that James Lambert and Richard Bennett were soldiers in the same Company under the command of Captain Guy Hamilton and the Regiment of Colonel John Slaughter, starting in Richmond, Virginia, in March 1781. James Lambert and Richard Bennett further agreed that Brigadier General Rufus Putnam was their commander later that year.

Richard Bennett was a neighbor of James Lambert and Richard was five years younger than James. When James was engaged in the Battles at Point Pleasant and Great Bridge, Richard Bennett was only 11 and 12 years of age, respectively. At the time James started is fourth tour of duty in 1779, Richard had just turned 16 years of age. For these reasons, it is reasonable to assume that Richard Bennett always looked up to his older soldier friend and neighbor who had already experienced four battles against Indians and the British. It seems understandable that Richard Bennett wanted to enlist in early 1781 in the same company with James Lambert. Since James Lambert's tour of two years ended in the middle of 1781 and Richard Bennett's tour of 18 months ended in late 1782, they would have served together in the same company and under the same leadership for approximately four months; specifically, March, April, May and June, 1781.

---

222   Ancestry.com - U.S. Pensioners, 1818-1872, Year Range 1848-1868 and Year Range 1858-1872, p. 1 for each of the 2 Ranges, http://search.ancestry.com/cgi-bin, on 4/11/2008.

Lafayette's Virginia Campaign (1781)

"It should be understood that in early 1781, Virginia had no regular continental army troops in the state—only Virginia militia. There were basically two corps, one under Brigadier General Thomas Nelson, Jr. operating on the north side of the James River, and a second corps under Brigadier General Peter Muhlenberg operating on the south side of the James River. Overall command of American forces in Virginia had been relegated to Major General the Baron von Steuben. Steuben had been left in Virginia by Greene, on his way to the south, to attempt to ensure that Virginia lived up to its promise to continue supplying the army in the south.

Incidentally, Peter Muhlenberg was a Lutheran minister (his father was instrumental in bringing the Lutheran Church to America) and it was he that stood at the pulpit saying, 'There is a time to pray and a time to fight, and that time has come now', while removing his preacher's robe to show his Continental Army colonel's uniform.

Being on the south side of the James River, it fell to Muhlenberg to deal with Arnold's force in Portsmouth. However, Muhlenberg's force was too small to attack, but it was sufficient to temporarily contain the British."[223]

In February 1781, George Washington, sensitive to the pleas of the Virginia Governor, ordered Major General Marquis de Lafayette south with a picked force of some 1,200 New England and New Jersey troops. As unit commanders he had Colonel Joseph Vose of Massachusetts, Lieutenant Colonel de Gimat, a very able Frenchman who had arrived in America with Lafayette, and Lieutenant Colonel Francis Barber of New Jersey.[224]

"Major-general Baron Steuben was then in Virginia, with Generals Muhlenberg, Weedon, Nelson, and others; but their forces being untrained militia, the commander-in-chief considered it necessary to send to their assistance a body of Continentals from his own army. The detachment was composed of twelve hundred of his best soldiers—Light Infantry—and the command he gave to Lafayette."[225]

---

223   The Revolutionary War Battle of Petersburg, Virginia, April 2003 lecture by Robert P. Davis to the Sons of the American Revolution - Richmond Chapter, pp. 2 and 3, http://www.vssr.org/speeches_articles/battle_of_petersburg.pdf, on 4/25/2008.

224   Lafayette's Virginia Campaign (1781), http://xenophongroup.com/mcjoynt/laf_va.htm, p. 4 of 26, on 4/25/2008.

225   Johnston, Henry P., The Yorktown Campaign and the Surrender of Cornwallis, 1781, Harper & Brothers, 1881, Chapter III, Cornwallis and Lafayette in Virginia, p. 32, http://www.questia.com, p. 1 of 1, on 4/26/2008.

"Lafayette, who was at Richmond when Cornwallis reached Petersburg, being now within Greene's department, had received orders from that general to halt and take command of all troops in Virginia, and defend the State. To this one object, from this time forth, he directed his entire attention; and his first anxiety was to make himself stronger. The nucleus of his force was his own detachment from the Northern army, Brigadier-generals Muhlenberg and Weedon, Virginia Continental officers, and Generals Nelson, Stevens, and Lawson, State brigadiers, were then, or recently had been, in different parts of the field with small and fluctuating bodies of militia; while Major-general Steuben, who had come south with Greene, was endeavoring to organize regiments for the Virginia line from recruits enlisted for eighteen months."[226]

"The Marquis de Lafayette took command of the Corps of Light Infantry on 20 February 1781. This Corps, on 29 April, was sent by Washington to reinforce Virginia. Lafayette's force arrived at Richmond and together with existing forces now totaled 3,550 men. The main strike element of the force included the light infantry companies of all of the Main Army's regiments which were stationed in the Hudson Highland's fortifications."[227]

The light infantry corps operating in Virginia included the 1st battalion which consisted of eight light Massachusetts infantry companies under the command of Colonel Vose, and two light Massachusetts infantry companies were assigned to the 2nd battalion under the command of Lt. Col. Gimat.[228]

In February 1781, the eight eldest companies of Massachusetts troops were formed into a battalion and placed under the command of Colonel Joseph Vose. This battalion was placed in Lafayette's Division and participated in the military operations in Virginia in 1781.[229]

The Massachusetts Line in 1781 consisted of ten infantry regiments, including the 1st Massachusetts Regiment commanded by Col. Joseph Vose and the 5th Massachusetts Regiment commanded by Col. Rufus Putnam.[230]

---

226   Ibid., p. 35.

227   The Company Informer, The Fifth Connecticut Regiment of the Continental Line, March, 2006, Connecticut's Light Infantry in the Yorktown Campaign By Edward L. Wittkofski, p. 2.

228   Ibid.

229   Yorktown Battlefield - Colonel Joseph Vose (U.S. National Park Service), http://www. nps.gov/york/historyculture/vosebio.htm, p. 1 of 1, on 4/26/2008.

230   The Continental Army of 1781, http://www.myrevolutionarywar.com/units-american/1781.htm, p. 3 of 6, on 4/26/2008.

The 5th Massachusetts Regiment was consolidated on 1 January 1777 with Walbridge's Company, 13th Continental Regiment, and the consolidated unit was redesignated as Putnam's Regiment, consisting of 8 companies. The 1st Massachusetts Brigade was relieved on March 31, 1778 from the Northern Department and assigned to the Highland's Department. The Regiment was reorganized on May 12, 1779 to consist of nine companies and redesignated as the 5th Massachusetts Regiment on August 1, 1779. The Regiment was relieved from the 1st Massachusetts Brigade and assigned to the 2nd Massachusetts Brigade on January 1, 1781.[231]

After a full day's forced march, Lafayette arrived at Richmond, Virginia, on the evening of 29 April 1781 with about 1,200 Continentals. The town had only a small corps of militia under General Thomas Nelson. This was only two days after the British had sunk the Virginia Navy vessels at Osbornes on the James River and just four days after the British defeated about 1,000 militia under Generals von Steuben and Muhlenberg at the Battle of Petersburg.[232]

With respect to the Battle of Petersburg, Virginia, on 25 April 1781, the following was reported:

"The withdrawal of the Virginia Militia was expeditious and quite orderly through the village of Blandford, across the valley and creek of Lieutenant Run, and onto the higher ground of the eastern edge of Petersburg. Muhlenberg's main line consisted of two more regiments of Infantry under Colonels Faulkner and Slaughter."[233]

It is interesting to note that the American units that fought in the Siege of Yorktown in October 1781 included the Light Division headed by Maj. Gen. Marquis de Lafayette. His 1st Brigade, led by Brig. Gen. Peter Muhlenberg, included Col. Vose's Battalion of 8 Massachusetts light companies and Lt. Col. Gimat's Battalion of 5 Connecticut, 2 Massachusetts, and 1 Rhode Island light companies. His 2nd Brigade, led by Brig. Gen. Moses Hazen, included Lt. Col. Scammell's Battalion of 2 New Hampshire, 3 Massachusetts, and 3 Connecticut light companies.[234] Thus, there were a total of 13 Massachusetts light companies engaged in the Siege of Yorktown.

231   5th Massachusetts Regiment, http://www.myrevolutionarywar.com/states/ma/ma-05.htm, p. 1 of 2, on 4/25/2008.

232   Lafayette's Virginia Campaign (1781), http://xenophongroup.com/mcjoynt/laf_va.htm, pp. 8 and 9 of 26, on 4/25/2008.

233   City of Petersburg "THE BATTLE OF PETERSBURG", http://www.petersburg-va.org/revwar/battle2.htm, p. 2 of 5, on 4/25/2008.

234   Yorktown order of battle - Wikipedia, the free encyclopedia, http://en.wikipedia.org/wiki/Yorktown_order_of_battle, p. 3 of 5, on 4/26/2008.

The diary of Ebenezer Wild, 1ˢᵗ Massachusetts Regiment, provides data on shelters used in 1781 on the march from West Point to Virginia, including operations against British forces in Virginia, Yorktown siege operations, and the march north to New York for winter cantonment. For the period between 19 February to 29 November 1781, the troops over a period of 285 days, spent 148 days or 51.9% in tents, 52 days or 18.3% in buildings, 51days or 17.9% in the open, 31 days or 10.9% on shipboard, and 3 days or 1.2% in makeshift shelters.[235]

After the Battle of Guilford Court House in North Carolina on 15 March 1781, it is my conclusion that Major-General Nathanael Greene led the Virginia Militia, including James Lambert, north through Hillsborough, North Carolina, into Virginia. James Lambert spent most of his time in western Virginia near Broadford; however, he also told us he was in the area of Richmond. It is my understanding that James' neighbor and younger friend, Richard Bennett, joined James Lambert's company in March 1781 in Richmond. The Virginia Militia top leadership in the area at that time included Major-General Nathanael Greene, Major-General Baron von Steuben, and Brigadier-General Peter Muhlenberg. James Lambert and Richard Bennett agreed that their Regiment was commanded by Colonel John Slaughter and their Company by Captain Guy Hamilton.

On 29 April 1781 Marquis de Lafayette arrived in Richmond with his northern troops from the Hudson Highland's Department, including the Massachusetts Regiments headed by Colonel Joseph Vose, Colonel Rufus Putnam and others.

James Lambert and Richard Bennett also agreed that they came under the leadership of Colonel Rufus Putnam.

Since James Lambert was discharged in June 1781 at the end of his tour of two years duration, it is apparent that James Lambert and Richard Bennett served together under this command leadership for only the months of March, April, May, and June, 1781. It appears that the primary assignments given James Lambert and Richard Bennett during this period of time was to protect public and private properties, including supplies for military operations.

---

235   Rees, John U., Analysis of American Soldiers' Campaign Lodging, 1776-1781, The Brigade Dispatch , vol. XXXII, no. 3 (Autumn 2002), pp. 7-10, http://www.revwar75.com/library/rees/shelteranalysis.htm, pp. 2 and 4 of 9, on 4/26/2008.

The Patriot Index of the Sons of the American Revolution includes Lt. Colonel John Slaughter, as a Patriot. The record indicates he was born in Culpeper County, Virginia, in 1732, and his parents were Francis Slaughter and Anne Lightfoot. He married Mildred (Milly) Coleman in Essex County, Virginia, in 1753/55, and their children were Robert and William. Mildred died 1 May 1758 (just 15 days after the birth of Robert) at the age of 22. John married his second wife, Elizabeth Suggett, in Richmond County, Virginia, on 18 December 1758. Their son, Thomas Keen Slaughter, was born of 11 October 1775. John Slaughter died in Virginia during the month of July 1796 at the age of 64.[236]

The Patriot Index of the Sons of the American Revolution also includes Major Andrew Hamilton, Sr., as a Patriot. The record indicates he was born in Augusta County, Virginia, on 2 May 1739. He married Jane McGill in Augusta County, in 1764, and their son, John, was born in 1766 in Abbeville, South Carolina. Andrew died at the age of 95 on 17 January 1835 in Abbeville, South Carolina, and his wife, Jane McGill, died on 20 April 1835 also in Abbeville, South Carolina.[237] More detailed data on Major Andrew Hamilton and his family was included in the material relative to James Lambert's 1st tour of duty (Battle at Point Pleasant) under the caption "Colonel Charles Lewis and the Augusta County Regiment."

Pension File No. R3551 on Captain Mark Finks of Madison County, Virginia, includes a certified supporting affidavit of William Yowell, Sr., dated 23 May 1834, which further documents the existence of Colonel John Slaughter's Regiment in 1781. This affidavit reads in part as follows:

"*. . . . that he has all his life been acquainted with Capt. Mark Finks of the County of Madison (then Culpeper County) that when he came of age to be placed upon the muster roll, that said Finks was then a Captain of Militia, which was during the Revolutionary War, that he knows by his own knowledge that said Finks was in service as Captain during the said War of the Revolution, on tour of duty, which, he thinks was not more than two months, but knows that it was not less than two months, that he the said Yowell was with Capt. Finks this tour, that the detachment he thinks mustered at Culpeper Court*

---

236   Family Group Record for John Slaughter (#), SAR Patriot Index Edition III Database, Copyright 1995-2002, National Society of the Sons of the American Revolution.

237   Family Group Record for Andrew Hamilton (#) Sr., SAR Patriot Index Edition III Database, Copyright 1995-2002, National Society of the Sons of the American Revolution.

House, and then marched to Fredg. Va. and joined the Regiment commanded by Col. John Slaughter and from thence marched and joined the main Army under Command of Genl. Muelenburgh below Petersburgh Virginia shortly after the enemy made his appearance in the neighborhood of where we lay, and our army retreated towards Petersburgh at which place we had an engagement, that Capt. Finks was then in Command of his Company upon that occasion. . . .and the said Yowell further states that he does not remember the year or time of the year when this service was performed."[238]

There is a map of American Revolution in the South, 1778-1781. It shows the battle locations James Lambert mentioned, such as, Camden and Cowpens, South Carolina, Guilford Court House, North Carolina, and Petersburg, Virginia. It also shows many of the towns and rivers James Lambert referenced in his pension application documents, including Richmond and Norfolk, Virginia; Hillsborough, Charlotte and Wilmington, North Carolina; as well as the James, Dan, Haw, Yadkin, Catawba, Pee Dee and Broad Rivers.[239]

---

238   Madison County, VA - Military - Captain Mark Finks, Revolutionary War Pension Application, http://ftp.rootsweb.ancestry.com, p. 4 of 6, on 4/25/2008.

239   Map of American Revolution in the South, 1778-1781, http://battleofcamden.org/nps7881.pdf, p. 1 of 1, on 5/13/2008.

DOCUMENTS IN JAMES LAMBERT PENSION FILE NO. R6099 SUBSEQUENT TO AMENDED DECLARATION OF JAMES LAMBERT (13 MAY 1844)

Amended Declaration of James Lambert for a Pension (21 August 1844)

On the 21st day of August 1844, James Lambert personally appeared before the Justice of the Peace, John T. Lavenson, at the Dearborn County Circuit Court, Lawrenceburg, Indiana, and said the following under oath:

"... saith that by reason of old age and the consequent loss of memory he cannot swear positively as to the precise length of his service but according to the best of his recollection he served not less than the periods mentioned below and in the following grades.

For three months I served as a drafted militiaman in the army of the revolution in the service of the United States.

For two years I served as a volunteer in the army of the revolution in the service of the United States, making in all Two years and three months, for which I claim a Pension 240

Letter to the Hon. O. B. Ficklin (6 June 1848)

On the 6th of June 1848, the Pension Office sent a letter to the Hon. O. B. Ficklin, House of Representatives, that read in part as follows:

"... James Lambert the other case referred to by Mr. Manly asserted a claim in 1842 for an alleged service in the militia of Virginia of 3 months, and for an enlistment of 2 years in the Continental Line. But he has furnished no satisfactory evidence in support of his application nor has he so specified his service as to enable us to make an examination of the Rolls of Virginia Line in this office for proof thereof."241

---

240   See Appendix, Item 4, p. 130.
241   See Appendix, Item 5, p. 132.

It would appear that Mr. Manly was representing James Lambert with respect to his pension application and the Hon. O. B. Ficklin of the United States House of Representatives had also requested an update on the status of the pension claim by James Lambert. Membership of the 30th Congress of the United States included from the State of Illinois Representatives Orlando Ficklin of District 3 and Abraham Lincoln of District 7.[242]

The background and experience of Orlando B. Ficklin is set forth below:

" . . . Orlando B. Ficklin . . . was born in Scott County, Kentucky, in December, 1808. His parents moved to Potosi, Missouri, when he was a boy and he attended the schools in Potosi until it became time for him to attend college, when he returned to Kentucky and entered old and historic Transylvania University in the City of Lexington. He also graduated from its law department. He decided to remove to Illinois, where he was examined for admission to the bar by Governor Edward Coles of Illinois. In 1829 he located in Mount Carmel, Illinois, and in 1832 was elected state's attorney for the district in which Wabash County was located. He was also elected colonel of the militia of that county and served under Gen. Milton K. Alexander in the Black Hawk war. In 1836 he was elected to the Legislature and there met Lincoln, Douglas and many other members who in later years became prominent men of Illinois. He was later elected to the Legislatures of 1837 and 1838.

The capital of the state at that time was Vandalia and these sessions of the Legislature were famous on account of the fight made by Lincoln and the six members from Sangamon County to move the capital to Springfield. Senator Beveridge, in his life of Lincoln, speaks of O. B. Ficklin as the brilliant Democratic leader in these Legislatures. He was elected to Congress in 1842 and served five terms (to 1852). Both Lincoln and Douglas were members during the time he was in Congress. The other members from Illinois were Long John Wentworth, Gen. John J. Hardin and Gen. John McClernand. He moved to Charleston, Illinois, in 1839, and lived there until his death in 1886. He presided at the Lincoln and Douglas debate held in Charleston, September 18, 1858, and as he had served in Congress the only time Lincoln was a member the latter called on him during the debate to state that he, Lincoln, had not voted against supplies to the soldiers during the Mexican war. He rode the circuit with Lincoln and tried many cases in which they were opposing counsel. The most famous was the Matson case. General Matson, a wealthy Kentucky slave owner, bought a large farm in Coles County, Illinois. He brought some of his Kentucky

242   Membership of the 30th Congress of the United States, http://borzoiblog.com/30th. htm, p. 3 of 13, on 3/28/2007.

slaves with him. He concluded to return to Kentucky and started to take his slaves with him. They, however, became free when they entered the State of Illinois and O. B. Ficklin was employed to get out a writ of habeas corpus to prevent them from being taken out of the state. Lincoln was employed by General Matson and argued the case in court against the former slaves. The trial lasted three days before two judges of the Supreme Court and was decided against Matson. This case settled the slave question in Illinois for ever. . . . He (O. B. Ficklin) was one of the great lawyers of the state and for twenty-five years or more was selected by the justices of the Supreme Court as chairman of the committee that examined candidates for admission to the bar. It is said his name appears in as many Supreme Court reports as any lawyer who ever practiced in the state. . . ."[243]

Letter from T. R. Young (5 Jan 1850)

On the 5th of January 1850, a T. R. Young wrote the Commissioner of Pensions, Colonel J. L. Edwards, stating in part the following:

"Have the kindness to afford me or my constituent Mr. Manly, another hearing in the case of James Lambler (Lambert), late of Indiana, under Act 7th June, 1832.

This case is represented to be a good one and should be allowed. If not allowed, be pleased to point out the reasons for its rejection. His children will renew the claim in the manner required by your Office . . . ."[244]

Timothy R. Young from Marshall, Illinois, served in the Thirty-First Congress from March 4, 1849 to March 3, 1851.[245] A brief biography on Congressman Young reads as follows:

"YOUNG, Timothy Roberts, a Representative from Illinois; born in Dover, N. H., November 19, 1811; completed preparatory studies; attended Phillips Exeter (N. H.) Academy and was graduated from Bowdoin College, Brunswick, Maine, in 1835; studied law in Dover, N. H., and was admitted to the bar; moved to Marshall, Ill., in the spring of 1838 and practiced law for ten years; elected as a Democrat to the Thirty-first Congress (March 4, 1849-March 3, 1851); moved to Mattoon, Ill., and became interested in the manufacture of plug tobacco, in which he continued for ten years; engaged in agricultural

---

243   Coles County, IL Biographies, http://genealogytrails.com/ill/coles/colebios.html, pp. 8 and 9 of 20, on 3/26/2007.

244   See Appendix, Item 6, p. 133.

245   THIRTY-FIRST CONGRESS, March 4, 1849, to March 3, 1851, p. 139.

pursuits near Casey, Clark County, Ill.; died at Oilfield, near Casey, Ill., May 12, 1898; interment in Marshall Cemetery, Marshall, Ill."[246]

Since the letters of June 6th, 1848 and January 5th, 1850, both made reference to the involvement of a Mr. Manly, further research was done in an effort to identify Mr. Manly. The 1850 United States Federal Census listed a lawyer named, Uri Manly, age 43, born in Massachusetts about 1807, residing with his wife, Lovina, two daughters and a son, in Marshall, Clark County, State of Illinois.[247] It is apparent that Uri Manly was representing James Lambert and his heirs in their efforts to obtain a pension and he was able to gain some political influence through his Illinois Congressmen; namely, Orlando B. Ficklin and Timothy Roberts Young. It is unknown at this time as to how an Illinois lawyer gained James Lambert and other Indiana residents as clients; however, it is known that the legal papers of the Hughes, Denver and Peck law firm in Washington, D. C. include a file with the label: "1864, Jan 31-1867 Manly, Uri (heirs)." The Hughes materials, 1833-1888, are legal papers from said law firm and the partners were James Hughes, 1823-1873, lawyer, congressman from Indiana, and professor of law at Indiana University, 1853-1856; James William Denver, 1817-1892, lawyer, general, congressman from California, and governor of Kansas Territory; and Charles F. Peck, lawyer from Illinois.[248]

On 11 June 2008, the compiler had the opportunity to review the file with the label: "1864, Jan 31 - 1867 Manly, Uri (heirs)" at the Lilly Library on the campus of Indiana University, Bloomington, Indiana.

This file contained a Petition by Dean Andrews, Executor of the Estate of Uri Manly, of Marshall, Clark County, Illinois. This Petition to the Court of Claims, Washington, D.C., stated that Uri Manly was a Captain and Assistant Quartermaster of Volunteers in the United States Army.

This Petition further stated that Samuel Applegate was hired as Pilot in the Quartermaster Department on the U. S. Transport "Leon" and that Samuel Applegate performed his services on the Arkansas River from January 1, 1864 to the date of his death on or about 6 February 1864. His monthly rate of pay was $375.00.

---

246   Timothy Roberts YOUNG – Infoplease.com, http://www.infoplease.com/biography/us/congress/young-timothy-roberts.html, p. 1 of 2, on 3/26/2007.

247   Ancestry.com - 1850 United States Federal Census, http://search.ancestry.com, p. 1 of 1, on 3/28/2007.

248   HUGHES MSS., http://www.indiana.edu/~liblilly/lilly/mss/html/hughes.html, pp.1 and 3 of 17, on 3/28/2007.

On or about 24 February 1864, Captain Manly authorized, with the approval of his superior officer, the payment of the net amount of $438.30 for Samuel Applegate's services to his brother, Josiah Applegate.

However, said payment was disallowed by the Third Auditors Office of the Treasury Department at Washington, D.C., for the reason that Disbursing Officers are not authorized to settle with heirs until the accounts have been passed upon by the Second Comptroller of the Treasury.

This file also contained an Affidavit by Burns Archer, a clerk in the Quartermaster Department at the time who was familiar with the details of this transaction, and said Affidavit was certified by Thomas W. Coles, Clerk of the Circuit Court, Clark County, Illinois, on 13 September 1867. This Affidavit contained the statement that Uri Manly died on 11 November 1864.

The Executor, Dean Andrews, was following the recommended procedure to petition the Court of Claims to seek reimbursement from the government for the disallowed payment of $438.30 which apparently had been charged to Captain Uri Manly's account. This file did not disclose the outcome of the Executor's efforts in this regard.

Unfortunately, this file gives us no further insight on how and why Uri Manly became involved in Jane Lambert's revolutionary war pension claim as the widow of James Lambert. However, we have learned that Uri Manly became a Captain in the Union Army; that he was stationed in or near Little Rock, Arkansas, in early 1864; and that he died on 11 November 1864 at 57 years of age. We have also learned that he was a caring person both as a lawyer and as an Union Army Officer in the Civil War. For example, he tried to be of service to others, including the heirs of James Lambert and Samuel Applegate. Further, we have learned that the heirs of Uri Manly also suffered the stress and frustrations, like the heirs of James Lambert, of trying to gain fair and timely treatment from the federal government relative to the military service of their ancestors.

Letter from Francis A. Dickins (19 Mar 1852)

On the 19th day of March 1852, Francis A. Dickins from Washington sent a letter to James E. Heath, Esq., Commissioner of Pensions, stating the following:

"Enclosed you will find the Amended Declaration of Thomas (James) Lambert under the Act 7ᵗʰ June 1832. Be as good as to have it filed with the original papers and the claim acted upon."[249]

Letter from Francis A. Dickins (31 Jan 1853)

On the 31ˢᵗ day of January 1853, Francis A. Dickins from Washington sent a letter to the Commissioner of Pensions, stating the following:

"In your letter you say that the amended declaration of James Lambert of Indiana, filed by me, only contained a restoration of his former declaration and you require some proof. On examination it will be found that a part of the service is proved certainly sufficient to entitle him to some pension. I must therefore request that the case may be re-examined and a pension allowed for such service as is proved."[250]

It is interesting to learn that Francis A. Dickins filed at least one of the 1844 Amended Declarations of James Lambert.

The Manuscripts Department of the Academic Affairs Library of the University of North Carolina at Chapel Hill has a long tradition for documenting the history and culture of the American South. One of the its collection names is "Francis Asbury Dickins Papers, #218, 1729-1934," and the descriptive entries for this collection reads as follows:

"Chiefly correspondence between the family of Dickins, planter of Ossian Hall in Fairfax County, Virginia, agent for the U. S. War and Treasury Departments, and lawyer of Washington, D. C., and the family of his wife, Margaret Harvey Randolph. Correspondence includes advice on the handling of slaves (1845); the purchase of two elderly slaves (1848); and a mention of post-Civil War servants in Virginia (1868)."[251]

The 1850 United States Federal Census listed a Francis A. Dickins, born in England about 1805 and residing with his wife, Margaret, three daughters and a son in Washington Ward 2, Washington, District of Columbia. The occupation listed for

---

249   See Appendix, Item 7, p. 134.
250   See Appendix, Item 8, p. 135.
251   Manuscripts Dept, UNC at Chapel Hill, http://www/upress.virginia.edu/epub/pyatt/ chap01.html, p. 25 of 103, on 3/28/2007.

Francis A. Dickins was "Agent for claimants" and the value of real estate owned was "$20,000."[252]

Power of Attorney (14 Mar 1854)

On the 14th day of March, 1854, the surviving widow of James Lambert, Jane Lambert, executed a Power of Attorney form before a Notary Public, Hamilton Conaway, in Dearborn County, State of Indiana. The witnesses to Jane Lambert's execution of this document were Hamilton Conaway and James Woods. This Power of Attorney appointed Charles C. Tucker of Washington City, D. C. as her true and lawful Agent and Attorney to examine and prosecute any Revolutionary Pension claim of her deceased husband.[253]

Charles C. Tucker was an Attorney and Agent for Claims in Washington, D. C. In 1854, he compiled a volume entitled: A List of Pensioners in the State of Massachusetts, Comprising Invalid Pensioners and Revolutionary Pensioners Under the Acts of Congress Passed March 18, 1818, May 15, 1828, and June 7, 1832.[254]

Letter from G. H. Voss (13 Jun 1855)

On June 13, 1855, G. H. Voss sent a letter from Noblesville, Hamilton County, Indiana, to the Hon. L. P. Waldo, stating the following:

"The Heirs of James Lambert say that he was a Revolutionary Pensioner-that he never drew any money but that a short time before his death say in 1847 the department wrote the old man that his application for back pay, and his pension dues-were all ready for him and all he had to do was to draw the same in the usual manner. The old man died before he could see to it, now they very much desire that you will say to them-whether the records show any thing due the old man, and if so what steps will be necessary on their part to draw the same. Advices at this place."[255]

Loren Pinckney Waldo was Commissioner of Pensions under President Pierce from March 17, 1853, until January 10, 1856, when he resigned to become judge of the superior court of Connecticut 1856-1863. He was born in Canterbury, Connecticut, February 2, 1802. He studied law and was admitted to the bar in 1825. He was elected

---

252   Ancestry.com - 1850 United States Federal Census, http://search.ancestry.com, p. 1 of 1, on 3/28/2007.

253   See Appendix, Item 9, p. 136

254   A List of Pensioners in the state Massachusetts - New England Historic Genealogical Society, http://newenglandancestors.org, p. 1 of 2, on 3/29/2007.

255   See Appendix, Item 10, p. 138.

as a Democrat to the Thirty-first Congress (March 4, 1849-March 3, 1851), serving as chairman, Committee on Revolutionary Pensions.[256]

The 1850 United States Federal Census lists a Gustavus H. Voss, born in Ohio about 1822 with a wife, Sarah A., and two daughters, residing in Noblesville, Hamilton County, Indiana. His occupation was listed as a lawyer and the value of owned real estate was $6,000.[257] G. H. Voss was also included in the Indiana Delegation to the 1868 Republican National Convention as an alternate delegate for the 5th District.[258]

Notes in the James Lambert Pension File No. R6099 suggest that the Bureau of Pensions took the following positions on the dates specified with respect to the status of the pension claim of James Lambert:

January 8, 1842. Claimant should specify tours.

January 13, 1845. Referenced letter of January 8, 1842 - service not specified.

June 6, 1848. No adequate proof of service - not specified service.

January 22, 1850. Original declaration returned for official seal.

June 28, 1852. 2nd Declaration merely reiteration.

Brief History on Department of Veterans Affairs

A brief history on the Department of Veterans Affairs reads as follows:

"American Colonies"

From the beginning, the English colonies in North America provided pensions for disabled veterans. The first law in the colonies on pensions, enacted in 1636 by Plymouth, provided money to those disabled in the colony's defense against Indians. Other colonies followed Plymouth's example.

256   WALDO,Loren Pinckney - Biographical Information, http://bioguide.congress.gov, p. 1 of 1, on 3/29/2007.

257   Ancestry.com - 1850 United States Federal Census, http://search.ancestry.com, p. 1 of 1, on 3/29/2007.

258   The Political Graveyard:Indiana Delegation to 1868 Republican National Convention, http://politicalgraveyard.com/parties/R/1868/IN.html, p. 1 of 2, on 3/29/2007.

In 1776 the Continental Congress sought to encourage enlistments and curtail desertions with the nation's first pension law. It granted half pay for life in cases of loss of limb or other serious disability. But because the Continental Congress did not have the authority or the money to make pension payments, the actual payments were left to the individual states. This obligation was carried out in varying degrees by different states. At most, only 3,000 Revolutionary War veterans ever drew any pension. Later, grants of public land were made to those who served to the end of the war.

In 1789, with the ratification of the U. S. Constitution, the first Congress assumed the burden of paying veterans benefits. The first federal pension legislation was passed in 1789. It continued the pension law passed by the Continental Congress.

In 1808 all veterans programs were administered by the Bureau of Pensions under the Secretary of War. Subsequent laws included veterans and dependents of the War of 1812, and extended benefits to dependents and survivors.

There were 2,200 pensioners by 1816. In that year the growing cost of living and a surplus in the Treasury led Congress to raise allowances for all disabled veterans and to grant half-pay pensions for five years to widows and orphans of soldiers of the War of 1812. This term later was lengthened.

A new principle for veterans benefits, providing pensions on the basis of need, was introduced in the 1818 Service Pension Law. The law provided that every person who had served in the War for Independence and was in need of assistance would receive a fixed pension for life. The rate was $20 a month for officers and $8 a month for enlisted men. Prior to this legislation, pensions were granted only to disabled veterans.

The result of the new law was an immediate increase in pensioners. From 1816 to 1820, the number of pensioners increased from 2,200 to 17,730, and the cost of pensions from $120,000 to $1.4 million.

When Congress authorized the establishment of the Bureau of Pensions in 1833, it was the first administrative unit dedicated solely to the assistance of veterans.

The new Bureau of Pensions was administered from 1833 to 1840 as part of the Department of War, and from 1840 to 1849 as the Office of Pensions under the Navy Secretary. The office then was assigned to the new Department of Interior, and renamed the Bureau of Pensions. In 1858 Congress authorized half-pay pensions *to veterans' widows and to their orphan children until they reached the age of 16."*[259]

Thus, James Lambert and Jane Lambert and their representatives were dealing with personnel in the Office of Pensions under the Navy Secretary between 1841 and 1849, and thereafter with personnel in the Bureau of Pensions under the Department of the Interior. It is easy to understand that the pension laws and procedures were very complex at that time and applicants for a pension, such as, James and Jane Lambert, were required to seek the assistance of knowledgeable specialists who also had political connections; primarily, lawyers and members of Congress.

After a though analysis of the James Lambert Pension File, one can better appreciate the time and persistent efforts James Lambert and Jane Lambert made in their attempts to gain the approval of his pension claim. One can hardly understand the frustrations in dealing with (1) the bureaucratic procedures of the Office of Pensions and the Bureau of Pensions from 1841 to 1855; (2) the need to hire well connected pension law specialists; and (3) such an arbitrary and prolonged period of a suspended or pending claim status. It had to be an enormous and unfair burden and hardship on James Lambert, a Revolutionary War soldier who had served three years during four tours of duty and had been engaged in at least four battles; namely, Point Pleasant, Great Bridge, Cowpens and Guilford Court House. He also was in his eighties at the time of this pension claim process.

Today, it seems rather hypocritical that some of the suspension and rejection letters from the Commissioner of Pensions, such as, J. L. Edwards, were signed:

"Your obedient servant".[260]

Revolutionary War Pension Lists - Rejected or Suspended Applications

In obedience to a resolution of the Senate of September 16, 1851, the Secretary of the Interior sent to the President of the Senate on February 16, 1852 a statement showing the names of all the applicants for pensions under the acts of June 7, 1832, July 4, 1836, and July 7, 1838, respectively, and the acts amendatory thereof, whose

---

259   History of the Department of Veterans Affairs - Part 1 - Public and Intergovernmental Affairs, http://www1.va.gov/opa/feature/history/history1.asp, pp. 1 and 2 of 4, on 3/29/2007.

260   Hugh Pierce Pension Application, http://www.zianet.com/jpierce/references/WarDept. html, p. 2 of 2, on 5/13/2008.

claims have been rejected or suspended, the grounds of such suspension or rejection, and the places of residence of such applicants, so far as the same can be given.[261]

The reprint of this rare United States Document lists the names and addresses of about 11,000 Revolutionary War soldiers and/or widows who applied for pensions and whose claims were rejected or suspended, along with the reasons. Most of the claims were for authentic service of actual Revolutionary soldiers but were rejected or suspended because the soldier did not serve for six months, his name did not appear on the rolls, or because a claim was suspended for further proof.[262]

Under suspended claims of Indiana residents, James Lambert is listed as a resident of Wilmington, Dearborn County, and the reasons for suspension were:

"Not on any rolls-no proof of service."[263]

Eighty-one (81) residents of Indiana are included in this listing of suspended claims.[264]

It is interesting to note that under rejected claims of Indiana residents a total of one hundred and twenty-seven (127) residents of Indiana are listed.[265]

Out of these 208 total suspended and rejected claims of Indiana residents, only one claim was considered to be fraudulent. This is evidence that 99.5% of these Indiana applicants were honest and truthful to the best of their abilities about their Revolutionary War service.

I whole heartedly agree with B. B. Moss who stated in his Preface of **_The Patriots at the Cowpens_** that:

---

261   32nd Congress, 1st Session, Senate, Ex. Doc. No. 37. Printed from Family Archive Viewer, CD145 Revolutionary War Pension Lists, Rejected or Suspended Applications for Rev. War, Secretary of the Interior Report. © The Learning Company, Inc., March 29, 2007.

262   Rejected or Suspended Applications for Revolutionary War Pensions: Genealogical Publishing Company, Baltimore, Maryland, © 1969, http://www.genealogical.com, p. 1 of 2, on 10/24/2006.

263   Printed from Family Archive Viewer, CD145 Revolutionary War Pension Lists: Rejected or Suspended Applications for Rev. War Claims of Indiana Residents, 1850, © The Learning Company, Inc., March 30, 2007, p. 413.

264   Ibid., pp. 411-414.

265   Ibid., pp. 406-410.

"I included the Rejected Claims because these claims were most often rejected because proper procedure was not followed or sufficient information was not submitted, not because the soldier did not perform the military service he claimed. Since fraudulent claims usually had been discovered, investigated, and removed from the files by the United States Government, I felt confident that the majority of the men whose claims were rejected reported truthfully their military activities. . . . I surmised that either lapses in memory or intervening years or both had caused the claimants to make a possible error."[266]

B. G. Moss made another important point which I also agree is accurate. He made the following statement:

"It should also be pointed out that the records of the militia units are scarce. Therefore many of the militiamen who fought under the militia officers at Cowpens may never receive the recognition they deserve."[267]

Revolutionary War Patriots Buried in Indiana

In 1938 the Indiana Daughters of the American Revolution published the "Roster of Soldiers and Patriots of the American Revolution Buried in Indiana", edited by Mrs. Roscoe C. O'Byrne. This publication was sponsored by the Indiana State DAR organization and all of its entries were considered to be authentic for membership in DAR.

In 1949 Margaret R. Waters compiled a listing of 300 additional names of Revolutionary soldiers who died, or were buried, in Indiana and whose names were not included in the 1938 DAR publication. The sole purpose of this compilation was to provide for descendants some helpful hints for their genealogical research. It was not intended as a supplement to the 1938 DAR publication.

In 1954 Margaret R. Waters also compiled a Supplement entitled: "Revolutionary Soldiers Buried in Indiana" which listed 485 soldiers who were not included in either the 1938 or 1949 publications. In searching for possible pensions for these 485 soldiers, Margaret R. Waters read 2,495 pension files and she abstracted 177 records, including the pension file records on James Lambert. The data she abstracted on James Lambert reads as follows:

---

266   Moss, Bobby Gilmer, The Patriots at the Cowpens, Revised Second Edition 1991, Scotia Press, (C) 1985 by B. G. Moss, p. viii.
267   Ibid., p. ix.

b. 3-25-1757, Md.; d. 5-13-1844; m. Jane ----. Pens. appl. on 11-18-1841, ae. 85 on 3-25-1842, Dearborn Co., Ind. After War, liv. Va.; Md.; Pa.; Ohio; Ind. Again appl. 5-13-1844, ae. 86 on 3-25-1844, Ripley Co., Ind., but a res. of Dearborn Co., Ind.; lives ca. 30 mi. from Lawrenceburg but only ca. 15 mi. from Versailles & it is a better road. Affid. 7-23-1841, Hamilton Co., O., of Lemuel Hungerford, ae. 79 last May 14, res. of Ross Twp., Butler Co., O.; that he & Lambert were in service at same time in same places. P of A, 3-14-1854, Dearborn Co., Ind., of wid., Jane Lambert. Service: first enl. June 1774, Wilson's Station in Tiger Valley on Monongahela River, in his 17th yr.; retd. to father at Wilson's Sta., again enl. first Sept. 1774 for 3 mo.; father mov. to N fork of Potomac in Rockingham Co., Va.; drf. in July 1775; Col. Hillyard, Capt. Spencer; in first appl. he says drf. ae 19, Augusta Co., Va., Mil.; Capt. Spencer, Maj. Guy Hamilton. REF: Pens. R.6099 Va.; Susp. Pens. List (1852) p. 413 - - not on any rolls - - no proof of service." [268]

Highlights from James Lambert Pension File

Having now made a detailed review of the James Lambert Pension File, it is clear that James Lambert highlighted for us the following pertinent facts about his life and his significant participation in the Revolutionary War:

- James Lambert was born on Pipe Creek, near Hagerstown, Maryland, on 25 March 1758.

- His age was recorded in the family record of his father's bible located in Nelson County, Kentucky, on 13 May 1844.

- His first military tour of duty was as a volunteer for three months in 1774 at age 16.

- His second military tour of duty was as a draftee for three months in 1775 at age 17.

- His third military tour of duty was for six months in 1776-1777 at ages 18-19 as a substitute for Jacob Ellsworth.

---

268   Waters, Margaret R., <u>Revolutionary Soldiers Buried in Indiana (1949), With Supplement (1954)</u>, Indianapolis 1949 and 1954, Reprinted for Clearfield Company, Inc., by Genealogical Publishing Co., Inc., Baltimore, Maryland 1992, 1999, p. 61.

- His fourth tour of duty was as a volunteer for two years in 1779-1781 at ages 21-23.

- Thus, James Lambert served a total of three years of service as a result of four military tours of duty, according to his Amended Declaration of 13 May 1844. However, he limited his claim for a pension to two tours of duty and a total of at least two years and three months of service in his Declaration of 18 November 1841 and his Amended Declaration of 21 August 1844.

- James Lambert was engaged in at least four battles of the Revolutionary War as a member of the Virginia Militia and Virginia Line.

(1) The defeat of the Indians in the first battle of the Revolutionary War at Point Pleasant, Virginia (now West Virginia), on 10 October 1774. His personal observation was that he *received several (musket) balls through his clothes.* His leaders included General Andrew Lewis, Colonel Charles Lewis, Major Andrew (Guy) Hamilton and Captain John Skidmore.

(2) The victory over the British at the Battle of Great Bridge, Virginia, on 9 December 1775. His leaders included Colonel William Woodford of the 2nd Virginia Regiment, Lt. Colonel Edward Stevens, and Captain Joseph Spencer. At the end of this tour he was discharged by Colonel William Crawford of the 5th Virginia Regiment.

(3) The victory against the British at the Battle of Cowpens, South Carolina, on 17 January 1781. His personal observations included the statement that *"one of my messmates, Thomas Warmsley, had the straps of his knapsack shot off and I had a (musket) ball strike my leg, but not to cause me to be laid-up, it was a flesh wound only, but I carry the scar to this day."* He also stated that he witnessed the effective use of a swivel cannon that literally split open a war medic. James Lambert's leaders at this battle included General Nathanael Greene, General Daniel Morgan and Colonel John Eager Howard.

(4) With respect to the pyrrhic victory of the British at the Battle of Guilford Court House, North Carolina, on 15 March 1781, James Lambert made specific reference to the fact the Brigadier General Edward Stevens was wounded, having been shot through his thigh. His leaders at this battle included General Nathanael Greene and Brigadier General Edward Stevens.

- With respect to his experience at West Point, New York, James Lambert informed us that the "cold winter" was in 1779-1780 and that he was engaged in the building of block houses. His leaders at this time included Captain Spencer at West Point, New York, Captain Cary at Horseneck, Connecticut, and Captain Adam Shapely at New London, Connecticut. The Statement of Lemuel Hungerford (23 July 1841) stated that he served under these same leaders with James Lambert.

- With respect to his service after the Battle of Guilford Court House, James Lambert gave us his personal observation of an attempt by the Americans to recover from the James River near Richmond, Virginia, some sixty brass cannons sunk by the British at Osbornes on 27 April 1781. At this time James Lambert's leaders included General Peter Muhlenberg, Colonel John Slaughter and Captain Andrew (Guy) Hamilton. As a result of the placement of the Massachusetts battalion under the command of Colonel Joseph Vose into Lafayette's Division, Colonel Rufus Putnam, commander of the 5th Massachusetts Regiment, also became one of the leaders of James Lambert's military unit. The documents in the Richard Bennett (Bennet) and James Lambert Pension Files document that these two soldiers were in agreement that they served together at this time under the same leadership.

- During his lifetime, James Lambert lived in Maryland, Pennsylvania, Virginia (West Virginia was not carved out of Virginia until 1863), Kentucky, Ohio and Indiana.

- James Lambert first entered service in 1774, then living with his father at Wilson Station, Virginia, in the Tiger (Tygart) Valley on the Monongahela River. His father moved in early 1775 to Rockingham County, Virginia, on the North Fork (South Branch) of the Potomac River. James lived with his father at this location until the close of the Revolutionary War in 1783. After 1783, James lived in Kentucky, Ohio and Indiana.

- James Lambert died in the late 1840s, probably in 1847 at the age of 89 as a resident of Dearborn County, Indiana, leaving a widow, Jane Lambert. It is most likely that he was buried in Dearborn County, Indiana.

- The James Lambert Pension Claim was considered by the pension authorities to be in a "suspended" status and the reasons for suspension were "Not on any rolls - No proof of service."

- However, it is clear that James Lambert was reputed and believed to be a Revolutionary War soldier by his family members, neighbors, community leaders and others.

- The Honorable James Duncan, sole Justice of the Ripley County, Indiana, Probate Court, having presided at the proceedings in the matter of the application of James Lambert for a Pension, rendered the Court's Opinion on 13 May 1844 that James Lambert was a Revolutionary soldier who served as he stated to the Court.

Conclusion of Compiler

As a result of this project over a period of ten years, it is my conclusion that the Honorable James Duncan, sole Justice of the Ripley County, Indiana, Probate Court, had it right when he rendered the opinion of the Court on 13 May 1844 that James Lambert was a Revolutionary soldier who served as he stated to the Court. In my opinion, my additional research has confirmed and verified the accuracy of the Court's opinion 164 years ago.

Index

Appendix

Item 1 - Statement of Lemuel Hungerford (23 Jul 1841)
Item 2 - Declaration of James Lambert (18 Nov 1841)
Item 3 - Amended Declaration of James Lambert (13 May 1844)
Item 4 - Amended Declaration of James Lambert for a Pension (21 Aug 1844)
Item 5 - Letter to the Hon. O. B. Ficklin (6 Jun 1848)
Item 6 - Letter from T. R. Young (5 Jan 1850)
Item 7 - Letter from Francis A. Dickins (19 Mar 1852)
Item 8 - Letter from Francis A. Dickins (31 Jan 1853)
Item 9 - Power of Attorney (14 Mar 1854)
Item 10 - Letter from G. H. Voss (13 Jun 1855)
Item 11 - Affidavit of James Lambert (3 April 1826)

ITEM 1

<u>Statement of Lemuel Hungerford (23 Jul 1841)</u>
(Transcription by George R. Lambert)

The State of Ohio   )

Hamilton County   ) SS

I Lemuel Hungerford of Ross Township Butler County and State Ohio being seventy nine years of age on the 14th day of May last having been first duly sworn according to the Law. Depose and say that I served in the revolutionary war between Great Brittain and the United States in the years of 1779 and 1780 as near as I can recollect in the militia under Captain Spencer at West Point and Captain Cary at Horse neck and Captain Adam Shapley at Newlondon where I saw Mr. James Lambert who resides in Dearborn County Indiana and who I have this day met and conversed with in Hamilton County, Ohio, serving at the above named places as a Militia Soldier in the revolutionary war at the time I was there serving as such myself and further deponent saith not.

His

Lemuel X Hungerford

Mark

The State of Ohio   )
Hamilton County   ) SS

Be it remembered that on this 23rd day of July A.D. 1841 personally appeared Lemuel Hungerford before me John Ashby a Justice of the Peace within and for said County and after having duly cautioned under oath to the foregoing deposition and subscribed the same in my presence. I also further certify that from information and all appearances he is a man whose character stands good for truth and veracity.

John Ashby (Seal)
Justice of the Peace

Declaration of James Lambert (18 Nov 1841)
(Transcription by George R. Lambert)

The following is the declaration of James Lambert a soldier of the Revolutionary War in North America.

The said James Lambert on this day personally appeared in the Probate Court of the County of Dearborn in the State of Indiana at the November Term of said Court 1841 it being a Court of Record created by the laws of Indiana and makes oath that on the 25 day of March 1842 he will be eighty five years old, that he was born in the State of Maryland, that he is now a resident of said County and has been for the 27 years last past, that he has lived in Virginia, Maryland, Pennsylvania, Ohio and Indiana, and in order to obtain the benefit of the Sessions pension laws he makes this further declaration, that at the age of nineteen at the town of Augusta in Virginia, he was drafted as a militia man for the term of three months, that he rendevous'd at Shenandoah, Virginia, and thence marched to Richmond, Virginia, and from thence was taken by water to West Point, New York, where when his term of three months expired he volunteered for the term of two years and after remaining there a winter and a summer he was marched to and was in the Battle of Cowpens and thence was marched to one of the Moravian towns on the Yadkin River where he was regularly discharged which he has lost that he served as aforesaid two years and three months in the army of the revolution, the reason why he never applied for a pension is that he never needed a pension until now, the name of his Major was Guy Hamilton, Captain name Spencer, Sergeants names John Walker, Hildepeny, William Bryan, Col. Hilliard or Hilyard, that his memory is defective and further says not.

His

James Lambert   X

Mark

Sworn to and subscribed
In Open Court November 18
1841 Wm. V. Cheek, Clerk
The State of Indiana   )
Dearborn County   )   SS

In the Dearborn County
Probate Court November
Term 1841

Be it remembered that on this day personally appeared in Open Court the within named James Lambert who made oath therein that the within declaration is true in substance and in matter of fact.

Witness: William V. Cheek, Clerk of
said Court and its seal this 18th November 1841

ITEM 3

Amended Declaration of James Lambert (13 May 1844)
(Transcription by George R. Lambert)

The amended Declaration of <u>James</u> <u>Lambert</u>.

In order to obtain the benefit of the act of Congress passed June 7, 1832.

State of Indiana   )
Ripley County   )   SS

On the 13th day of May 1844, personally appeared in Open Court before the Hon. James Duncan sole Justice of the Ripley County Probate Court in and for the County of Ripley and State of Indiana, <u>James</u> <u>Lambert</u>, a resident of the County of Dearborn in the said State aged Eighty-Six years the 25th day of March 1844. (And the reason assigned why this applicant makes this Declaration as aforesaid in the County of Ripley instead of the County of Dearborn where he resides is this to wit. He lives about thirty miles from Lawrenceburg the present County seat of Dearborn where the Courts of said County are holden, and he resides not more than fifteen miles from this Court, the Road from his residence to this Court is much better than to Lawrenceburg, and he is wholly dependent on the kindnesses of his neighbors for the means of coming to Court to make his declaration and it was much easier for him to get a friend to bring him to this Court than take him to Lawrenceburg) And the applicant being first duly sworn according to law doth on his oath make the following declaration in order to obtain the benefit of the Act of Congress passed June 7, 1832.

That he entered the service of the United States under the following named officers and served as herein stated. The first of June 1774 (or near that time) he volunteered for <u>three</u> <u>months</u>, and served against the Indians under Col. Lewis, Maj. Hamilton, Capt. Skidmore, Lieut. Col. Rafe Stewart and Ensign William White, 1st Sergeant James Stewart, a brother to Lieut. Col. Stewart, and marched from Wilson Station which was situated in Tiger Valley on the Monongahela River to the mouth of the Kanawha River where he was in a severe engagement with the Indians about three hundred whites were killed and wounded but how many of the Indians could not be ascertained as the warriors to save the scalps of the fallen would drag them to the Ohio and throw them into the stream. This battle was a hard one, the Indians were defeated, but with great loss to the whites. Sergeant Stewart was killed and this applicant received several balls through his clothes. This engagement commenced near sunrise and lasted all day. He served for full three months when he returned home to his father at Wilson Station, this was in his seventeenth year and the first of September 1774 or in a few days of that time at all events he served full three months when he was verbally discharged.

His father now removed from Wilson Station and settled on the North Fork of the Potomac in Rockingham County, Va., and this applicant went also with him and continued to make his father's house his home until after the close of the Revolution only when he was in the army.

In the month of July 1775 he was drafted for three months, and entered the service under the command of Col. Hillyard, Capt. Spencer, 1st Lt. Hilldepeny and Corporal John Walker the rest of his officers names he has forgotten. He was marched to Richmond and served for full three months when he was discharged in October 1775 by Capt. Spencer.

He remained at home for one month when he entered the service a third time. He entered as a substitute for six months for one Jacob Ellsworth. He was doing this tour of six months under the command of Col. Hillyard, Maj. Hamilton (he thinks), Capt. Spencer, Ensign William Bryan, Sergeant Hilldepeny (the rest of his officers names he has forgotten) but applicant is not certain but what he served this tour or a part of the same under a Maj. White. Applicant may also be mistaken as to the precise year when this tour was rendered but it was the same year that the engagement called the Scrimmage of the King's Bridge. He was in that engagement and it was in his three months tour before his six months tour as a substitute for Ellsworth or in this six months tour and the department must decide the year from that fact. In all events he served his tour of six months and was discharged in writing by Col. Hillyard.

He again entered the service as a volunteer for two years in the Spring of 1779 and served in the Company of Captain Andrew Johnson, when after having served for some time in that Company he was transferred to the command of Capt. Christman, and he also served in another Company the Capt. name forgotten. During this tour of two years he was under the Command of Genl Gates who commanded in the South, and also under the command of Genl Greene after the fall of 1780. He was also under the command of Col. Hillyard, Col. White, Col. Woods, Col. Morgan, Col. Dorathy and several Brigadier Generals amongst whom he remembers Genl Stevens who was wounded at the Battle of Guilford. He remembers also Col. Lynch. He also remembers in the Company he last served, or during his tour of two years Maj. Guy Hamilton, Lieut. Robert Morris and Ensign Murphy. He continued in the service until after the Battle of Guilford when he was discharged in May or June 1781 after having faithfully served two years this last tour as a volunteer added to his three tours before, to wit three months against the Indians in 1774 and three months when he was drafted, and six months as a substitute for Jacob Ellsworth makes <u>Three years</u> which he served. He served four tours as follows. Three months as a volunteer, three months was drafted, six months as a substitute for Jacob Ellsworth and two years as a volunteer, and he resided then at the time of his first tour in Wilson Station on the Monongahela River in Tiger Valley then he removed to Rockingham County, Va., on the North Fork of the Potomac and resided there during the War. He was in the Battle with the Indians at the mouth of the Kanawha on the Ohio, in the engagement or Battle at Kings Bridge where about 300 British were engaged, and during his tour of two years he was in the Battle of the Cowpens in January 1781 and also in the Battle of Guilford Court House in March 1781. He was also about ten miles from Camden when that Battle was fought he was engaged in doings in Bienes, and was not in the engagement but in hearing of it.

During his first tour against the Indians, he was marched from Wilson Station through the wilderness under the guide of one Joseph Friend, and also one Capt. Frogg who commanded in the Right wing at the Indian Battle, and was killed in that engagement. He crossed Cheat River, Laurel Fork and Glady Fork to Kanawha and down the same to the mouth, he returned nearly the same route.

2<u>nd</u> Tour. He marched from the North fork of the Potomac in Rockingham County to the Shenandoah in Loudon County. There he remained for about ten days until more troops collected, which were then expected from Greenbrier and Jackson River. The troops arrived under the command of Col. Johnson and they took up their line of march for Richmond from Loudon, they marched to Pages at Swift Run Gap from thence to New Castle from thence to Richmond where he remained for one month then he marched to Manchester where he remained about one month then he marched to Rocky Ridge where he returned home to Rockingham.

3<u>rd</u> Tour. He marched from Rockingham to New Castle, from thence to Richmond were he remained he cannot say how long from thence to Manchester, from thence to a small town about twenty or thirty miles as near as he can remember down James River from Richmond from thence he marched to Norfolk where he remained until he was discharged by Col. Crawford. He then returned home and remained until the Spring of 1779 when he volunteered for two years.

4<u>th</u> Tour. He marched to Richmond was quartered in the Capitol, stayed there for about three months, was engaged in frequent Scouts, took shipping at Rockets Landing two miles from Richmond and went to Norfolk stayed there several weeks cannot say how long-from thence he went to West Point on the North river, quartered there the winter of 1780 (the cold winter) and was engaged in building Block Houses. He sailed from Norfolk for West Point in the fall of the year. From West Point he marched to Horse neck on the East River where he remained for three months, went from Horse neck to Peekskill, from thence marched to Virginia, got there at time cherrys were ripe. Marched over Haw River on to North Carolina. The object was to secure General Gates who was there in the south. He marched across Dan River, Deep River and Peedee and was quartered at Ruduly (Rugeley) Mill, Ruduly (Rugeley) was said to be a Tory. He there helped to take out flour for the American army. After the Battle of Camden he joined the army of the southern commander Gates at Hillsborough, N. C. There he remained for several weeks when he went to Charlotte and well remembers when Genl Greene addressed the command of the South which was in the fore part of the winter before the Battle of Guilford and the Cowpens. This applicant cannot pretend to give in detail all that happened during this part of his service. He was frequently engaged in foraging parties and in scouts and was in many places the names of which he cannot remember. He was marched to the Cowpens in January 1781 and was there in that Battle. He there saw Col. Hillyard he thinks riding along the line with one arm hanging down shattered by a musket ball. He will also mention one circumstance somewhat suspicious. A warmedic was engaged in doing something to a man that had fallen by the shot of the enemy. He was in the attitude of stooping and a Ball from a Swivel struck him on a straight line and literally split him open. One of my messmates Thomas Warmsley had the straps of his knapsack shot off and I had a ball strike my leg, but not to cause me to be laid up, it was a flesh wound only, but I carry the scar to this day.

From the Cowpens we marched with the prisoners there taken about 300 in number for Virginia and it was understood that Lord Cornwallis was in pursuit of the forces under the command of Morgan. He joined the main army under Genl Greene near a river called Bannister River and marched direct for Guilford, N. C. It was some time after this before the Battle of Guilford was fought as much as two or three weeks. Here he marched and counter marched for some days in hearing of the enemy until in March 1781 (the day he does not remember) the Battle was fought. Here the enemy kept the field but immediately retreated leaving some of their wounded. The enemy marched for their shipping at Wilmington. After this Battle he was again at Hillsborough and from thence he marched to Broad ford on Adkin River and remained there for some time how long he cannot state but he was there discharged and returned with many more of the Virginia Militia back to their homes. This tour of two years he served out his time in full and was honorably discharged by Col. Hillyard in writing. That discharge has since been lost by being in the possession of one William Bennett who was drowned about a year afterwards. This applicant may possibly be mistaken in the names of some of his officers but he distinctly remembers during his said last tour of two years Genl Washington, Genl Greene, Genl Stevens, Col. Morgan, Col. Washington, Col. Howard, Col. White, Col. Lynch, Doudman, Williams, Jr. Sr. He will mention one thing more, when he was at Richmond he saw the Americans using a diving bell to recover the Brass Canon which the British had sunk said to be Sixty.

Applicant will here state that in his original Declaration for Pension made some two years since, he did not know that it was necessary to give a detailed statement of his services, and he is not certain whether he set down all of his tours of service, depending on his agent to inform him of the necessary precission. That he may have made some statements which may conflict with some things in this his narrative of his services, but if such is the case, he is not at fault with any design or intention to misinform the Commissioner of Pensions. He is a weak and feeble old man, and but a short time to enjoy any munificence or bounty of this government. What he has stated within as to the main facts and length of time which he served in the War of the Revolution are substantially true-And he claims it his duty to state further that one reason why he delayed so long in making application for a pension under the Act of June 7th, 1832 is, he has lived in a situation where he knew little of his rights. He had but few opportunities of seeing persons who could give him correct information about Pensions, and had conceived the idea some how, that he must produce his discharge which he could not do. He has no documentary evidence, and he knows of no person whose testimony he can produce, who can testify to his services.

He hereby relinquishes any claim whatever to a pension or annuity except the present, and declares that his name is not on the pension roll of any agency of any State.

His
James X Lambert
Mark

Sworn to and subscribed in Open Court the day and year first above written.

Conrad Overturf, Clerk

By: John S. S. Hunter, Deputy

Mr. John Ruby — a clergyman residing in the County of Ripley and State of Indiana and I. W. Robinson residing in the said County and State do hereby certify that we are well acquainted with James Lambert who has subscribed and sworn to the above Declaration, that we believe him to be Eighty Six years of age, that he is reputed and believed in the neighborhood where he resides to have been a soldier of the Revolution, and that we concur in that opinion.

Sworn to and subscribed the day and year aforesaid.

John Ruby (s)
Isaiah W. Robinson (s)

And the said Court do hereby declare this opinion, after the investigation of the matter, and after putting the interrogatories prescribed by the War Department that the above named applicant was a Revolutionary Soldier and served as he states. And the Court further certifies that it appears to him that John Ruby who has signed the preceding certificate is a clergyman resident in the County of Ripley and State of Indiana, and that I. W. Robinson who has also signed the same is a resident in the County of Ripley and State aforesaid and is a credible person and that their statement is entitled to credit.

James Duncan, P. Judge (Seal)

I, Conrad Overturf, Clerk of the Ripley County Probate Court do hereby certify that the foregoing contains the original proceedings of said Court in the matter of the application of James Lambert for a pension.

In testimony whereof I have hereunto set my hand and the seal of said Court at Versailles this 13th day of May 1844.

Conrad Overturf, Clerk
By: John S. S. Hunter, Deputy

Answers to the questions propounded by the War Office to applicant for Pension under Congress Act of June 7th 1832.

1st Question Answered.

I was born on Pipe Creek near Hagerstown, Md., on the 25th day of March 1758.

2nd Question Answered.

I have the record of my age in Nelson Co., Kentucky, in the Family Record in the Bible of my father.

3rd Question Answered.

When I was called into service during my first tour against the Indians, at Wilson Station in Tiger Valley on the Monongahela. I then removed to Rockingham County, Va., on the Potomac and resided there during the whole war. Since then I have resided in Kentucky and Ohio until for the last fourteen years since which I have resided in Dearborn Co., Indiana, where I still reside.

4th Question Answered.

The first tour I volunteered, the second I was drafted. The 3rd tour I served as a substitute for Jacob Ellsworth and the last was fourth tour I volunteered.

5th Question Answered.

I well remember the Riflemen commanded by Genl Morgan (or Col. Morgan at that time) also the Cavalry commanded by Col. Washington, also Col. Howard Regiment and Col. Lee and Col. Lynch-also I well remember of Col. Nock Regiment of Militia and the Company of Capt. Morton. The general circumstances of my service I have stated within.

6th Question Answered.

I received a written discharge at Broad ford on Adkin River signed by Col. Hillyard and it was lost as stated within on the person of William Bennett.

7th Question Ans. ?

Amended Declaration of James Lambert (21 Aug 1844)
(Transcription by George R. Lambert)

The Amended Declaration of James Lambert for a Pension under the act of Congress on the 7th day of June 1832 which original Declaration is now on file in the War Office of the United States.

State of Indiana   )
Dearborn County)   SS

On this 21st day of August 1844 personally appeared before me the undersigned a Justice of the Peace in and for the said County James Lambert, a resident of said County of Dearborn and State of Indiana who being first duly sworn according to law deposeth and saith, that by reason of old age and the consequent loss of memory he cannot swear positively, as to the precise length of his service, but according to the best of his recollection he served not less than the periods mentioned below, and in the following grades.

For three months I served as a drafted militiaman in the army of the Revolution in the service of the United States.

For two years I served as a volunteer in the army of the Revolution in the service of the United States, making in all Two years and three months, for which I claim a Pension. And the said deponent further saith that he knows of no person living by whom he can prove his said services, and that he has no written or documentary evidence by which he can prove the same.

His

James X Lambert

Mark

Sworn and Subscribed before me the day and year first above written.

John T. Lavenson, (s) (Seal)

State of Indiana   )
Dearborn County   )   SS

I, William V. Cheek, Clerk of the Dearborn County Circuit Court in and for the said County and State do hereby certify that John T. Levenson before whom the foregoing proceedings were had in the matter of the application of James Lambert for a Pension was at the time of hearing the same, and now is, an acting Justice of the Peace in and for the said County duly commissioned and qualified, that full faith is due and Credit should be given to all of his official acts, and that the foregoing Signature purporting to be his is Genuine.

In witness whereof I have hereunto set my hand and affixed the seal of said Court at Lawrenceburg this 16th day of November 1844.

William V. Cheek, (s) Clerk,
Dearborn Circuit Court

Item 5

Letter to the Hon. O. B. Ficklin (6 Jun 1848)
(Transcribed by George R. Lambert)

Pension Office
June 6th, 1848

Sir:

...

James Lambert the other case referred to by Mr. Manly, asserted a claim in 1842 for an alleged service in the militia of Virginia of 3 months, and for an enlistment of 2 years in the Continental Line. But he has furnished no satisfactory evidence in support of his application nor has he so specified his service as to enable us to make an examination of the Rolls of the Virginia Line in this office for proof thereof.

Hon. O. B. Ficklin
        House of Reps

Item 6

Letter from T. R. Young (5 Jan 1850)
(Transcribed by George R. Lambert)

Washington
January 5th, 1850

Sir:

Have the kindness to afford me or my constituent Mr. Manly, another hearing in the case of James Lambler (Lambert), late of Indiana, under Act of 7th June, 1832. This case is represented to be a good one and should be allowed. If not allowed, be pleased to point out the reasons for its rejection. His children will renew the claim in the manner required by your Office.

...

I am, Sir
Most respectfully,
Your O B Sevt
T. R. Young (s)

Col. J. L. Edwards
Comm. of Pensions

Item 7

Letter from Francis A. Dickins (19 Mar 1852)
(Transcribed by George R. Lambert)

Washington
19 March 1852

Sir:

Enclosed you will find the Amended Declaration of Thomas (James) Lambert under the Act of 7th June 1832. Be as good as to have it filed with the original papers and the claim acted upon.

Yours respectfully,

Francis A. Dickins.

James E. Heath, Esq.
        Comm. Of Pensions

ITEM 8

Washington
31 January 1853

Sir:

In your letter you say that this amended declaration of James Lambert of Indiana, filed by me, only contained a restoration of his former declaration and you require some proof. On examination it will be found that a part of the service is proved certainly sufficient to entitle him to some pension. I must therefore request that the case may be re-examined and a pension allowed for such service as is proved.

Yours respectfully,

Francis A. Dickins (s)

To the Commissioner of Pensions.

ITEM 9

Power of Attorney (14 Mar 1854)
(Transcribed by George R. Lambert)

Power of Attorney

Know all men by these presents: That I, Jane Lambert, surviving widow of James Lambert, deceased at Dearborn, State of Indiana, do hereby constitute and appoint Chas. C. Tucker, of Washington City, D.C., my true and lawful Agent and Attorney to prosecute the claim of my deceased husband for me for any amount of Revolutionary Pension or increase of Pension that may be due under the provisions of the Act of 1853 or any other Act or Resolution of Congress, and I hereby authorize my said Attorney to examine all papers and documents in relation to said Claim on file in the Departments at Washington City, or elsewhere, to file additional evidence or arguments, and to receive the Certificate which may be issued for said Claim, and to appoint one or more substitutes under him for the purposes herein expressed: and to do all things that I might or could do, were I personally present. Hereby ratifying and confirming all that my said Attorney may lawfully do in the premises.

Her

Jane   X   Lambert

Mark

WITNESS my hand and seal this 14 day of March 1854.
In presence of
Hamilton Conaway)
James Woods   )   SS

State of Indiana, Dearborn County—SS

On this 14th day of March 1854, before me a Notary Public in and for the County and State above mentioned personally appeared Jane Lambert the above named and acknowledged the foregoing power of Attorney to be her act and deed for the purpose therein mentioned.

Given under my hand and Notarial
Seal this the 14th day of March 1854.
Hamilton Conaway (s)

State of Indiana)

Dearborn County)   SS

On this 14 day of March 1854, before me the undersigned a Notary Public in and for the County and State aforesaid, personally appeared Jane Lambert a resident of said County, and made oath according to the law that she is the identical person who executed the foregoing power of Attorney, and that she is directly interested in said Claim, and makes this affidavit to be filed with such additional evidence or arguments as my said Attorney may use in prosecuting said Claim.

Her
Jane   X   Lambert
Mark

Sworn to and subscribed before me the day and year above written.

Given under my hand and Notarial Seal March 14th, 1854.

Hamilton Conaway (s)
Notary Public

ITEM 10

<u>Letter from G. H. Voss (13 Jun 1855)</u>
(Transcribed by George R. Lambert)

Noblesville, Hamilton County, Indiana
June 13, 1855

Hon. L. P. Waldo

Sir:

The Heirs of James Lambert say that he was a Revolutionary Pensioner - That he never drew any money but that a short time before his death-say in 1847- the department wrote the old man that his application for back pay, and his pension dues-were all ready for him and all he had to do was to draw the same in the usual manner. The old man died before he could see to it, now they very much desire that you will say to them-whether the Records show any thing due the old man, and if so what steps will be necessary on their part to draw the same.

Advice at this place.

G. H. Voss

Item 11

Affidavit of James Lambert (3 April 1826)
(Transcribed by George R. Lambert)

State of Indiana   )
Dearborn County)   SS

Before me Daniel Hagerman a Justice of the Peace in and for said County personally came James Lambert and on his oath states that Richard Bennett and this deponent enlisted at the same time at Richmond in the State of Virginia during the War under Captain John Slaughter, that they were afterwards attached to the Second Regiment of United States infantry under the command of Col. Guy Hamilton and Brigadier Gen. Rufus Putnam–that they enlisted in the year of 1781– during the war–that they served together in the same ranks until the close of the war, and at that time they were discharged, that afterwards they served a tour of duty as militia men, and were also discharged from those services–and further states that he is perfectly acquainted with the services of Richard Bennett and that he was Honorably, discharged and further saith not.

Sworn to and Subscribed to before me this 3rd day of April 1826.

His
James   X   Lambert
Mark

Daniel Hagerman, (s) JP

State of Indiana   )

Dearborn County)   SS

I, James Dill, Clerk of the Dearborn Circuit Court do hereby certify that Daniel Hagerman before whom the foregoing affidavit of James Lambert was subscribed and sworn to and subscribed and who has certified the same was at the time thereof and now is a Justice of Peace in and for the county of Dearborn and full faith and credit are due to all his official acts as such.

In testimony whereof I have hereunto affixed the mutilated seal of our said Court; (the said seal having been injured by fire on the night of the 5th of March 1826).

3rd of April 1826,

James Dill (s). Clerk